HEALTHCARE ACTIVE LEARNING

HAL

LEGAL ASPECTS OF HEALTH CARE

Start date

Target completion date

Tutor for this topic

Contact number

USING THIS WORKBOOK

The workbook is divided into 'Sessions', covering specific subjects.

In the introduction to each learning pack there is a learner profile to help you assess your current knowledge of the subjects covered in each session.

Each session has clear learning objectives. They indicate what you will be able to achieve or learn by completing that session.

Each session has a summary to remind you of the key points of the subjects covered.

Each session contains text, diagrams and learning activities that relate to the stated objectives.

It is important to complete each activity, making your own notes and writing in answers in the space provided. **Remember this is your own workbook—you are allowed to write on it**.

Now try an example activity.

ACTIVITY

This activity shows you what happens when cells work without oxygen. This really is a physical activity, so please only try it if you are fully fit.

First, raise one arm straight up in the air above your head, and let the other hand rest by your side. Clench both fists tightly, and then open out your fingers wide. Repeat this at the rate of once or twice a second. Try to keep clenching both fists at the same rate. Keep going for about five minutes, and record what you observe.

Stop and rest for a minute. Then try again, with the opposite arm raised this time. Again, record your observations.

Suggested timings are given for each activity. These are only a guide. You may like to note how long it took you to complete this activity, as it may help in planning the time needed for working through the sessions.

Time taken on activity

Time management is important. While we recognise that people learn at different speeds, this pack is designed to take 15 study hours (your tutor will also advise you). You should allocate time during each week for study.

Take some time now to identify likely periods that you can set aside for study during the week.

	Mon	Tues	Wed	Thurs	Fri	Sat	Sun
am							
pm							
eve							

At the end of the learning pack, there is a learning review to help you assess whether you have achieved the learning objectives.

LEGAL ASPECTS OF HEALTH CARE

Bridgit Dimond MA LLB DSA AHSM

Barrister-at-law and Emeritus Professor, the University of Glamorgan

THE OPEN LEARNING FOUNDATION

CHURCHILL LIVINGSTONE
EDINBURGH HONG KONG LONDON MADRID MELBOURNE NEW YORK AND TOKYO 1995

CHURCHILL LIVINGSTONE
Medical Division of Pearson Professional UK Limited

Distributed in the United States of America by Churchill
Livingstone Inc., 650 Avenue of the Americas, New York,
N.Y. 10011, and by associated companies, branches and
representatives throughout the world.

First published 1995

ISBN 0 443 05359 6

British Library of Cataloguing in Publication Data
A catalogue record for this book is available from the
British Library.

Library of Congress Cataloging in Publication Data
A catalogue record for this book is available from the
Library of Congress

Produced through Longman Malaysia,TCP.

For The Open Learning Foundation

Director of Programmes: Leslie Mapp
Series Editor: Robert Adams
Programmes Manager: Kathleen Farren
Design and Production: Steve Moulds

For Churchill Livingstone

Director (Nursing and Allied Health): Peter Shepherd
Project Manager: Valerie Burgess
Project Development Editor: Mairi McCubbin
Design Direction: Judith Wright
Copy Editor: Joanna Smith
Sales Promotion Executive: Maria O'Connor

CONTENTS

OPEN LEARNING FOUNDATION TEAM MEMBERS

Writer: Bridgit Dimond MA LLB DSA AHSM Barrister-at-law
Emeritus Professor,
University of Glamorgan

Editor: Diane West

Reviewers: Jan Williams
Chief Executive, Llanelli/Dinefwr NHS Trust, Prince Philip Hospital

John Tingle
Director, Centre for Health Law, Nottingham Law School

Series Editor: Robert Adams
OLF Programme Head,
Social Work and Health and Nursing,
University of Humberside

The views expressed are those of the team members and do not necessarily reflect those of The Open Learning Foundation.

The publishers have made all reasonable efforts to contact the holders of copyright material included in this publication.

THE OPEN LEARNING FOUNDATION

Higher education has grown considerably in recent years. As well as catering for more students, universities are facing the challenge of providing for an increasingly diverse student population. Students have a wider range of backgrounds and previous educational qualifications. There are greater numbers of mature students. There is a greater need for part-time courses and continuing education and professional development programmes.

The Open Learning Foundation helps over 20 member institutions meet this growing and diverse demand – through the production of high-quality teaching and learning materials, within a strategy of creating a framework for more flexible learning. It offers member institutions the capability to increase their range of teaching options and to cover subjects in greater breadth and depth.

It does not enrol its own students. Rather, The Open Learning Foundation, by developing and promoting the greater use of open and distance learning, enables universities and others in higher education to make study more accessible and cost-effective for individual students and for business through offering more choice and more flexible courses.

Formed in 1990, the Foundation's policy objectives are to:

- improve the quality of higher education and training

- increase the quantity of higher education and training

- raise the efficiency of higher education and training delivery.

In working to meet these objectives, The Open Learning Foundation develops new teaching and learning materials, encourages and facilitates more and better staff development, and promotes greater responsiveness to change within higher education institutions. The Foundation works in partnership with its members and other higher education bodies to develop new approaches to teaching and learning.

In developing new teaching and learning materials, the Foundation has:

- a track record of offering customers a swift and flexible response

- a national network of members able to provide local support and guidance

- the ability to draw on significant national expertise in producing and delivering open learning

- complete freedom to seek out the best writers, materials and resources to secure development.

Other titles in the series

INTRODUCTION

Why study health care law?

If you work in health care your activities are constrained by the legal framework within which you work. Whether you are a health professional or manager, or if your work is in a related area, your actions should be influenced by the law which gives rights and duties to employees. You cannot always rely upon obtaining legal advice; some decisions must be made on the spot.

Some of the reasons for studying health care law that might be applicable to you are given below.

1 To know when expert legal advice is essential and must be brought in.

2 To have an understanding of the legal rights of the patient as compared with moral/ethical rights.

3 To ensure that the correct procedures are laid down in a variety of situations, such as:

- abortion
- the registration of births, deaths and stillbirths
- the setting of standards of care
- the handling of complaints
- health and safety procedures.

4 To understand what action should be taken to prevent or minimise the possibility of litigation or complaints arising.

5 To take precautions to ensure that if litigation does arise you have an understanding of:

- standards of record-keeping
- procedures and policies
- training
- communications.

6 To know your rights as an employee.

7 To know the rights and duties of the employer and the duties of a manager.

8 An awareness of the significance in legal terms of codes of professional conduct.

9 To have enough legal understanding to be sure of handling outside bodies effectively, for example:

- community health councils
- the press
- the police
- MPs
- social services departments
- the Ombudsman.

Decisions often have to be made urgently – such as those regarding the disclosure of patient information and the involvement of others.

10 To know the rights against and duties towards trespassers and the duties of an occupier.

11 To understand some of the main legal terms in order to communicate more effectively with lawyers.

12 To know how to protect vulnerable persons such as children and mentally disordered people. It is necessary to know the rights of parents and others over them and when they can be challenged, especially in the context of non-accidental injury and consent to blood transfusions.

13 To be familiar with the law relating to health and safety; to have an understanding of the main ways of improving standards of health and safety provision and of obtaining compensation should harm arise. All employees are vulnerable to dangers at work and there are specific hazards associated with working within a health care context. In addition, staff need to know the legal implications of the risk of HIV infection and AIDS, their right to be protected from such risks and whether they can refuse to work.

14 Knowledge of the law brings with it an understanding of its strengths and deficiencies. This enables professionals and managers to press for changes where appropriate.

Litigation in health services has increased and is increasing, as can be seen from the figures provided by the Association for the Victims of Medical Accidents in its annual reports. In one sense this is a result of the success of health care. People today expect their treatment to succeed. If it does not, or if something goes wrong, then people can feel that there should be compensation and legal advice is sought. Often, however, people are simply seeking an explanation for what has happened, and when this is not immediately forthcoming they fear that negligence has occurred and suspect a cover up.

Anyone who works in health care whether public or private and in whatever capacity – manager, professional or support worker – must therefore be aware of the possibility of litigation occurring. In a vast industry it is not surprising that one of the biggest causes for criticism by the Health Service Commissioner is the weakness and failure in communications. If harm occurs as a result of failure in communication, this too can be a cause of litigation and compensation being awarded.

The scope of this unit

Health service law is a vast subject and it is impossible to cover all the topics within the 40 hours of study time allocated for this unit. The aim is to provide a basic understanding of the main laws which underpin health care and the work of the professional. Once this basic understanding is achieved the student can use it as a foundation for further study of other areas of concern or interest to him or her. The text book which accompanies this unit, *Speller's Law Relating to Hospitals* (Finch, 1994), is referred to throughout as *Speller*. It covers far more subject areas and in far greater depth than there is time for in this unit, and can be used to explore topics in greater detail at a later date. Specialists such as finance managers, supplies officers or any of the specialists within health care can supplement the work of the unit with further research in their specialist area using *Speller*.

This also applies to those non-NHS employees who are studying this course. As far as the statutory framework is concerned, the unit covers the aspects relating to the NHS. Anyone working outside the NHS, however, whether in a private or voluntary hospital, nursing home or other institution, will find a great deal that is relevant to their work both in the unit and in *Speller*. The law regarding patients' rights in relation to consent, confidentiality, access to records and so on is the same whether the patient is in NHS or non-NHS accommodation. The private patient does, however, have an additional potential cause of action since there is a contract between himself and the health professional which is not present in NHS care.

About *Speller*

Dr Speller was one of the earliest members of the Institute of Hospital Administrators (now known as the Institute of Health Service Management) and his book, first published in 1947, is the authority on health service law. It has been revised several times by different authors since Speller himself died. The author of the current edition is John Finch, a lecturer in law at Leicester University, an examiner for the Institute of Health Services Management and a well-known authority on health service law. The new edition includes the law relating to NHS trusts and the changes brought about by the NHS and Community Care Act 1990. *Speller* is a reference book – do not, therefore, try to read it through. Dip into it and refer to it for any problems and issues that concern or interest you. It is essential that you grasp the broad principles of law rather than get bogged down in the detail. This unit will assist you in this and will guide your reading and initial study.

About the unit

There are a number of activities in each session of the unit, each with a suggested time allowance which should be used as a guide only. In addition, there are suggestions as to other activities you may wish to undertake, such as observing meetings and visiting courts. Although these are entirely optional, they are extremely useful and you are urged to make the time to do them.

Cases and statutes are not given their full reference in the unit as these can be found in *Speller*. There are listings of these on pp. xxxii to lxxii before the main body of the text.

To avoid the use of cumbersome alternatives, 'he' and 'his' have been used throughout the unit to include 'she' and 'her'. This follows the style of UKCC publications, amongst others, and there is no intention to convey any other assumption or attitude.

The emphasis of this unit is on developing an understanding of the framework, main legal concepts and language of the law, and on exploring the basic principles of law which arise in health care. Note that we are concerned only with the law in England which also applies to Wales. Scotland and Northern Ireland have separate legal systems which are not covered in this unit.

Session One
Establishes the framework of accountability as it affects the health care professional through the criminal, civil and employment law and through the standards of the profession. It discusses in detail the principles of negligence and liability, both direct and vicarious.

Session Two

Examines the contract of employment and discusses the rights and obligations that are either expressly stated or understood by law to be inherent in the contract. It also discusses the role of trade unions in the health service.

Session Three

Discusses the law governing health and safety in the workplace and brings together the four areas of accountability which regulate health and safety in the health services.

Session Four

Looks at how consent for treatment and research is obtained, including the question of advance directives and the legal position when a patient is a minor or unable to give consent. Also discussed is the issue of allowing a patient to die by the withdrawal of treatment.

Session Five

Explores the duty of confidentiality and the issue of whistle-blowing. It looks at the law in relation to the keeping of records under the Data Protection Act 1984, as well as access to manual health records and medical reports.

Session Six

Looks at the statutory framework that governs the administration and internal procedures of the health services. It also explores the handling of complaints including the role of the Health Service Commissioner and the Mental Health Act Commission.

Session Seven

Examines the legal issues relating to the property of staff, patients, their visitors and the health service body itself, including the making of wills by patients.

Session Eight

Discusses the law governing the treatment and care of mentally disordered patients, including the role of managers in hearing appeals for discharge.

Session Nine

Looks at a variety of specialist areas such as organ transplant and the notification of infectious diseases. The unit ends with an activity which encourages you to keep abreast of future developments in health care law.

Preparation in advance

As the emphasis of this unit is the development of an understanding of the fundamental principles of law and the application of these principles within the practical arena, many of the activities require you to obtain information and publications from a variety of sources. Some of this collection might cause delays to your progress through the unit, so a summary of everything you will need is given below. You are recommended to make arrangements to obtain any materials you do not possess as soon as possible so that, hopefully, you will have everything you need when you tackle the activities.

Court visits

It is recommended that you visit a criminal, civil or coroner's court or an industrial tribunal or proceedings relating to professional conduct. If you can, find out the days when cases are being heard and arrange to visit. The court clerks are usually both helpful and informative concerning procedure.

Materials required for activities

For the following activities you will need to obtain copies of:

Session 1

Activity 1

- the code of professional conduct relating to your profession
- your contract of employment.

Activity 5

- any protocols or procedures which define standards of care within your own specialty.

Activity 8

- leaflets and other notices given to patients offering advice from departments such as accident and emergency, orthopaedic and plaster rooms, or even the leaflets which are given to patients on or before admission which set out details about arrangements for property and so on.

Session Two

Activity 9

- your contract of employment
- access to the *Whitley Council Handbook* if applicable to your job.

Activity 10

- the disciplinary procedure for your workplace.

Activity 11

- policies prepared by your employer relating to employees, including those on discrimination, disabled employees, and staff development and training. Supplement these with the advisory leaflets produced by the Employment Department on all aspects of employment.

Activity 12

- your employer's policy or declaration in relation to redundancy.

Activity 13

- details of the constitution, function, membership rules and services of your trade union from the local shop steward
- two booklets produced by the Employment Department: *Union Membership and Non-membership Rights* (PL 871 (REV3)) and *Industrial Action and the Law* (PL 943)
- your contract of employment.

Session Three

Activity 14

- a list of the current publications produced by the Health and Safety Commission from your local office of the Health and Safety Executive; also any leaflets covering the role of the Health and Safety Commission, the Health and Safety Executive and the Health and Safety Inspectorate.

In the text preceding this activity, there is a list of health and safety regulations covering six topics, one of which you will be asked to study for this activity (apart from the management of health and safety at work). You will need to obtain a copy of the Health and Safety Executive booklet on your chosen area of study.

Activity 15

- The Control of Substances Hazardous to Health Regulations (COSHH) from HMSO.

Activity 17

- your contract of employment.

Session Four

Activity 21

- consent-to-treatment forms used in your hospital.

Activity 25

- the procedure and practice of your local research ethics committee.

Session Five

Activity 26

- your local procedure for dealing with staff concerns; this should have been prepared as recommended in the NHS Management Executive's (1993) *Guidance for Staff on Relations with the Public and the Media* (reproduced as Resource 5 at the back of this unit).

Activity 28

- the Data Protection Registrar's annual report and the pack of information relating to the Data Protection Act, the regulations and the role of the Registrar.

Activity 30

- the document entitled *Standards for Records and Record Keeping* from the United Kingdom Central Council for Nursing, Midwifery and Health Visiting (UKCC, 1993).

Session Six

Activity 32

- *Managing the New NHS – A Background Document* (DoH, 1993a); this deals with the abolition of regional health authorities in the NHS.

If you are unable to attend a meeting of a joint consultative committee, as suggested in the text, try to obtain the papers relating to their meetings.

Activity 33

- the annual report of your local community health council.

Activity 34

- the NHS trust application for your hospital

- the NHS contract for the trust

- the annual report of the trust

- any documents which the community health council has prepared on the local situation.

If you work outside the NHS, try to obtain the comparable documents from your employers.

Activity 35

- the complaints procedure of your local hospital

- the annual report on complaints compiled for your hospital or trust.

Session Seven

Activity 40

- the procedure laid down by your hospital or unit for the protection of the property of patients and staff.

Activity 41

- any procedures or guidelines about the making of wills prepared by your hospital or unit.

Session Eight

Activity 43

- the Mental Health Act 1983

- the revised *Mental Health Act Code of Practice* prepared by the Department of Health (DoH, 1993b).

Activity 45

- *Community Supervision Orders* (Health Committee of the House of Commons, 1993) from HMSO

- *Legal Powers on the Care of Mentally Ill People in the Community*, Report of the Internal Review (DoH, 1993c)

- any new legislation on the subject of the care of mentally ill people in the community that has been enacted since this unit was published.

Activity 46

- the booklet, *Hearing Patients' Appeals Against Continued Compulsory*

Detention (Williamson, 1991), published by the National Association of Health Authorities and Trusts.

Session Nine

Activity 48

- *Midwives Rules* (UKCC, 1991a)

- *A Midwife's Code of Practice* (UKCC, 1991b)

- *Code of Professional Conduct* (UKCC, 1992).

Activity 51

- the *British National Formulary* (BNF) which provides information on medicines and will be available in your hospital pharmacy and may also be in the library.

LEARNING PROFILE

Given below is a list of learning outcomes for each session in this unit. It is not intended to cover all of the details discussed in every session and so it should only be used for general guidance.

For each of the learning outcomes listed below, tick the box that corresponds most closely to your current understanding. This will provide you with an assessment of your current knowledge and confidence in the areas that you will be studying in this unit so that you can set targets for your learning.

	Not at all	Partly	Quite well	Very well

Session One

I can:

- explain the basic technical legal terms and the framework of the civil and criminal legal system ☐ ☐ ☐ ☐

- describe the basic principles of accountability ☐ ☐ ☐ ☐

- discuss the relationship between codes of professional conduct and legal duties and powers ☐ ☐ ☐ ☐

- specify the circumstances which can lead to legal action being taken ☐ ☐ ☐ ☐

- minimise the risk of litigation through sound practices ☐ ☐ ☐ ☐

- summarise the defences which may be available. ☐ ☐ ☐ ☐

	Not at all	Partly	Quite well	Very well

Session Two

I can:

- define a contract of employment ☐ ☐ ☐ ☐
- summarise the legal rights of employers and employees ☐ ☐ ☐ ☐
- discuss the implementation of employment policies at my workplace ☐ ☐ ☐ ☐
- describe procedures for redundancy and the legal rights of trade unions. ☐ ☐ ☐ ☐

Session Three

I can:

- summarise the main provisions of the Health and Safety at Work Act 1974 regarding the appointment and duties of safety representatives ☐ ☐ ☐ ☐
- discuss specific health and safety regulations applicable in my workplace ☐ ☐ ☐ ☐
- apply the health and safety regulations to my workplace and take preventative measures in relation to health and safety ☐ ☐ ☐ ☐
- specify the key stages in the assessment of risk ☐ ☐ ☐ ☐
- discuss measures to promote the creation and maintenance of a health and safety culture ☐ ☐ ☐ ☐
- discuss the enforcement provisions for health and safety in the health services ☐ ☐ ☐ ☐
- relate health and safety to professional and contractual responsibilities ☐ ☐ ☐ ☐
- give illustrations of legal liability for health and safety. ☐ ☐ ☐ ☐

Session Four

I can:

- discuss the duty to inform the patient, supported by the authority of legal cases ☐ ☐ ☐ ☐
- describe the different methods of gaining consent and what constitutes consent ☐ ☐ ☐ ☐
- explain the circumstances when treatment can be given without the patient's consent ☐ ☐ ☐ ☐

	Not at all	Partly	Quite well	Very well

Session Four *continued*

- give an account of the legal principles regarding consent to treatment which apply to specific categories such as children and mentally disordered people

	☐	☐	☐	☐
highlight the problems inherent in advance directives and suggest solutions	☐	☐	☐	☐
discuss the withdrawal of treatment in the best interest of the patient	☐	☐	☐	☐
explain the principles and procedures regarding the use of patients for teaching and research.	☐	☐	☐	☐

Session Five

I can:

debate the issue of 'whistle-blowing' in the light of the NHS Management Executive's guidelines	☐	☐	☐	☐
discuss the duty of confidentiality and summarise the circumstances in which it does not apply	☐	☐	☐	☐
describe the main provisions of the Data Protection Act 1984	☐	☐	☐	☐
explain the statutory rights of access to health records held in manual form and to medical reports prepared for employment or insurance purposes	☐	☐	☐	☐
specify the legal requirements relating to the ownership and preservation of records.	☐	☐	☐	☐

Session Six

I can:

describe how the internal market works and debate the provision of health care	☐	☐	☐	☐
discuss the administrative structure of the health service and the function of the statutory authorities	☐	☐	☐	☐
summarise the advisory and consultative machinery which supports a dialogue between professionals and the authorities, and across different kinds of authority	☐	☐	☐	☐
give an account of the role of community health councils	☐	☐	☐	☐
outline the mechanism to regulate the relationship between purchasers and providers	☐	☐	☐	☐

	Not at all	Partly	Quite well	Very well
Session Six *continued*				
● discuss the procedures for the handling of complaints	☐	☐	☐	☐
● define the role of the Health Service Commissioner and the Mental Health Act Commission.	☐	☐	☐	☐

Session Seven

I can:

	Not at all	Partly	Quite well	Very well
● discuss liability for the property of staff, patients and their visitors	☐	☐	☐	☐
● specify the procedure that should be adopted when a patient wishes to draw up a will	☐	☐	☐	☐
● explain the restrictions on search and arrest by employers or managers.	☐	☐	☐	☐

Session Eight

I can:

	Not at all	Partly	Quite well	Very well
● explain the law regarding the detention and treatment of mentally disordered patients	☐	☐	☐	☐
● describe the regulation of leave of absence under the Mental Health Act 1983	☐	☐	☐	☐
● discuss the issues of guardianship and care in the community	☐	☐	☐	☐
● detail the duties of managers including that of hearing appeals for discharge	☐	☐	☐	☐
● explain the circumstances in which treatment can and cannot be given under the Mental Health Act 1983.	☐	☐	☐	☐

Session Nine

I can:

	Not at all	Partly	Quite well	Very well
● discuss the legal and professional responsibilities that are specific to midwives	☐	☐	☐	☐
● describe the legal position with regard to organ transplant and the use of the body after death	☐	☐	☐	☐
● identify the legal position regarding abortion and the registration of births and deaths	☐	☐	☐	☐
● explain the legislation in the area of medicines and poisons	☐	☐	☐	☐

	Not at all	Partly	Quite well	Very well

Session Nine *continued*

- summarise the aims of the Human Fertilisation and Embryology Act 1990 and discuss issues raised by developments in genetic research ☐ ☐ ☐ ☐
- describe the procedures to be followed when a notifiable disease or case of food poisoning is diagnosed. ☐ ☐ ☐ ☐

SESSION ONE

The framework of accountability

Introduction

This session is designed to give you an understanding of the legal framework and legal accountability within which health care professionals and other people involved in health care work. We will be looking at:

- the nature and source of the law

- the differences between criminal and civil law

- the principles of personal, criminal and civil liability

- accountability to the professional registration bodies

- the vicarious liability of the employer

- the various defences available to a defendant in the civil courts in an action for negligence.

Session objectives

When you have completed this session, you should be able to:

- explain a range of technical legal terms

- describe the framework of our civil and criminal legal system

- show an understanding of the basic principles of accountability

- specify the four elements that must be shown in an action for negligence

- define when and how an employer can be vicariously liable for the action of an employee

- summarise the defences which may be available should action be brought

- effect ways of minimising the risk of litigation through sound practices.

1: Accountability

Getting to grips with the jargon

First of all, let's look at some of the legal terms that will be used in this unit.

Civil action describes a law case brought by a person or organisation against another such body relating to the non-criminal law.

Criminal law is that which pertains to the prosecution of offences. There is not necessarily any intrinsic difference between a civil wrong and a criminal wrong: the former can be followed by civil proceedings, the latter by criminal proceedings, but some actions are both civil and criminal. A person who assaults another person, for instance, can be sued in the civil courts for compensation as well as being charged with an offence and prosecuted in the criminal courts. The criminal courts also have the power to award compensation to the victim.

Plaintiff is the term which describes the person bringing a civil action. This is usually the person who has suffered harm, but where that person has died then it is the representative of the deceased. Where the person harmed is under a disability such as a mental disorder or he is a minor, then he would be represented by his parent, guardian or another appointed person.

Cause of action is the justification in law recognised by the court that must be established before a case can be brought in the civil court. This may, for example, be a case of negligence, nuisance, breach of statutory duty, defamation and so on. Each cause of action has recognised elements which must be proved. The burden is on the plaintiff in the civil courts to prove, on a balance of probabilities, that the defendant is liable, by showing that each of the required elements is established through the evidence. In an action for negligence, for example, the plaintiff has to show the four elements set out in *Figure 1*. If the plaintiff fails to show each of these elements, then the defendant will win the case.

1	There is a **duty of care**

2	There has been a **breach of the duty of care**

3	This was **reasonably foreseeable** ...

4	and resulted in **Harm**.

Figure 1: The four elements in an action for negligence

The **defendant** is the person sued by the plaintiff. It is not always clear initially who should be the defendant. We will be discussing this issue later in this session.

To **sue** means to bring legal action against some person or body in the civil courts.

A **tort** is a civil wrong (excluding breach of contract) which enables the person who has suffered the wrong to claim compensation.

A **tortfeasor** is a person who has carried out a civil wrong and may therefore become the defendant in an action brought by the person who has suffered the wrong.

What is meant by 'the law'?

'The law' is the term that refers to the rules which are enforceable in society.

Statutory law

Some laws, known as 'statutory law', originate by Act of Parliament (in Great Britain: the House of Commons, the House of Lords and the Crown; in Europe: a decision of the European Parliament). Statutory law includes statutory instruments (SIs) which are the directions of a government minister and are known as 'delegated legislation'. Some statutory laws impose mandatory duties on those to whom they are addressed. Thus, under section 1(1) of the National Health Service Act 1977, the Secretary of State has a duty to continue the promotion of a comprehensive health service in England and Wales. This is a mandatory duty, although the section and subsequent sections give her discretion in how this duty is to be performed. Other statutes are enforced through the criminal courts, an example of which is the Health and Safety at Work Act 1974 which is considered in Session Three.

Common law

As well as statutory law, there is 'common law'. This is the law which derives from the decisions by judges in the courts of law. These decisions create precedents which should be followed by subsequent judges in cases based on similar facts. A recognised hierarchy of the courts determines which courts have to follow which precedents. Thus, the House of Lords is not bound to follow the decisions of any other court in the United Kingdom, even its own decisions, though it should only refuse to follow its previous decisions on exceptional occasions in order to give certainty and consistency to the implementation of the law. The House of Lords is, however, bound by those decisions of the European Courts which relate to legislation within the European Community.

Arenas of accountability

Health professionals face accountability for their actions in four different ways, through:

- criminal law
- civil law
- employment law
- professional registration.

Criminal law

They might have to answer before the criminal courts if they have committed an offence. Where a patient has died in suspicious or unnatural circumstances, the coroner might decide to hold an inquest and he can call upon anyone likely to have relevant information to prepare a statement and come before him as a witness. There may subsequently be criminal proceedings relating to the death. The implications of the criminal law in the field of health and safety will be considered in Session Three.

Civil law

Where a person claims compensation and has a cause of action which is recognised in the civil law, litigation can be commenced against the employer of the individual who is responsible for the harm or infringement of liberty. The principles applying in negligence will be considered later in this session. Where treatment is given without consent and there is no legal justification, then this would be a trespass to the person and gives a right of action for compensation in the civil courts. This will be considered in Session Four.

Employment law

Each employee has a contract of employment even if this has not been put in writing. The contract places duties upon the employee, some of which will be agreed by the parties as well as others which are known as implied duties, i.e. they are implied by the law relating to contracts. The employee has an implied duty, for example, to obey the reasonable orders of the employer and also to act with reasonable care and skill. Where the employee is in breach of this duty he may be disciplined and, in serious cases, dismissed. If he has the requisite length of continuous service, the employee could challenge the dismissal in an industrial tribunal. This will be considered along with disciplinary procedures in Session Two.

Professional registration

A registered professional who has to be on the register held by the appropriate registration body can also face the possibility of being struck off from the register which would mean that he would be unable to work as a registered professional until he was reinstated. The United Kingdom Central Council for Nursing, Midwifery and Health Visiting, the General Medical Council, the General Dental Council and other professional bodies hold professional conduct committee hearings to determine whether the professional has been guilty of misconduct. They also issue codes of professional conduct for the guidance of their registered members. These codes do not have the force of law, but can be used in evidence to show whether, in the view of the profession, the individual was following the standards of professional conduct.

ACTIVITY I   ALLOW 10 MINUTES

Obtain a copy of the code of professional conduct which relates to your profession, and identify the clauses which you think could be paralleled by comparable duties in the civil law, the criminal law and in your contract of employment. If you do not have a copy of the written statement of your contract of employment, ask the personnel department for a copy.

Note that a number of activities in this unit require you to obtain documents or other information. In order to give you a chance to do this before reaching the activity, a full list of the material required is given in the Introduction.

Commentary

All four arenas of accountability specify duties which are owed to patients, fellow employees and others, and impose responsibilities upon the professional and the manager for which sanctions are available in the event of non-compliance. As you work through this unit, the link between these various areas of accountability will become more evident.

The UKCC *Code of Professional Conduct for the Nurse, Midwife and Health Visitor*, for example, requires that professionals:

'1 act always in such a manner as to promote and safeguard the interests and wellbeing of patients and clients;

2 ensure that no action or omission on your part, or within your sphere of responsibility, is detrimental to the interests, condition or safety of patients and clients.'

(UKCC, 1992)

If, therefore, as a result of a serious error in the administration of drugs, for instance, a patient dies, the nurse could face:

● criminal proceedings for causing the death of the patient

● civil action brought by the relatives to obtain compensation for the death of the patient

● professional conduct proceedings by the UKCC

● disciplinary proceedings by the employer which could result in dismissal.

If the nurse is taken off the register, there would have to be a dismissal from the post of a registered practitioner.

2: Liability

Criminal liability

The courts are showing increasing reluctance to hold defendants liable for manslaughter when a person dies as a result of negligence during the performance of their duties. The House of Lords has recently ruled on the criteria to be applied.

Read *Speller*, section 6.2, pp. 149-153.

ACTIVITY 2	ALLOW 15 MINUTES

Turn to *Resource 1* at the end of this unit and read the Law Report entitled, '*Proving involuntary manslaughter*' (*The Times*, 1994).

Answer the following questions:

1 What decision had already been made?

2 What was the ruling in the House of Lords?

3 What reasons were given?

4 What is the significance of this decision for health service professionals?

5 What are your thoughts about the case?

Commentary

Not all cases of negligence where a death results will lead to a conviction for manslaughter. In this case, an anaesthetist had been convicted of manslaughter by the crown court for the death of a patient during an operation. He appealed against the conviction to the Court of Appeal and failed. He then appealed to the House of Lords. *Resource* 1 gives the summary of the decision of the House of Lords which was to uphold the verdict of the crown court.

Once negligence has been established (and in this case it was conceded by the defendant), the next stage in a criminal prosecution is for the jury to decide if there was gross negligence which would be a crime. This is dependent upon the seriousness of the breach of duty committed by the defendant in all the circumstances pertaining at the time. The Lord Chancellor set out exactly what the jury would have to consider.

This decision is important in clarifying the law and should assist health professionals and those with related interests in understanding whether an action of negligence could result in both civil and criminal proceedings, or only the former.

Liability in civil law

Most actions by patients are brought on the grounds of negligence by health professionals in relation to the care of patients. Someone contemplating such an action would have to obtain legal advice as to whether there is a *prima facie* (i.e. at first sight) cause of action. The burden is on the plaintiff to show the elements of a negligence action which were given in *Figure 1*. The plaintiff also has to decide who is to be the defendant, i.e. who is liable?

ACTIVITY 3 — ALLOW 10 MINUTES

A patient is admitted into an NHS trust hospital for surgery to repair a hernia. Unfortunately, by mistake, a swab is left inside the patient who has to return to theatre for a second operation. He is now claiming compensation for the additional pain and suffering, and for the extra length of time he was off sick and unable to return to work. It was established that the consultant failed to request that a swab count be taken and, because the theatre was under pressure, the nursing staff did not delay the end of the operation.

Which of the following do you think could be liable to pay compensation?

1 The person who caused the harm to arise?

2 The health authority which purchased the care from the NHS trust?

3 The NHS trust which employed the person in 1 above?

4 The members of the NHS trust board?

5 The immediate managers of the person in 1 above?

6 Any others?

Commentary

If harm is caused by the negligence of one person (on these facts it could be the consultant surgeon or the senior nurse), that person can be personally sued.

However, this is unlikely to occur because health authorities and trusts now accept responsibility for the negligence of all professional staff whom they employ. Health authorities had previously not been responsible for the actions of medical and dental staff, but this arrangement, which had existed since 1954, ended in 1990 with the acceptance of crown indemnity (this is discussed later in this session). Where an employee is negligent, the employer can be sued because of the employer's indirect liability, known as 'vicarious liability' (see below), for the negligence of an employee whilst acting in the course of employment. Thus, rather than suing **1**, the plaintiff would probably sue **3**.

Under the provisions of the NHS and Community Care Act 1990, the NHS trust is liable for the negligence of its staff, and therefore the health authority would not be liable to pay compensation. The situation would be different, however, where the health authority had not commissioned specific services from the trust and the plaintiff brings a claim in respect of the non-provision of services. The plaintiff would have to argue that the health authority had failed to fulfil its statutory duty of arranging for the provision of health care.

Members of the trust board are not personally liable for the harm which occurred (see *Speller* section 2.5.4, pp. 48-49), but the board can sue and be sued in its own right as a statutory body. The board, as the employer vicariously liable for the harm caused by the negligence of its employees whilst acting in the course of employment, could be sued in this example.

Managers are personally responsible for their actions but if they have delegated and supervised appropriately and are not at fault, they would not be held responsible in civil law for the negligence of their staff.

Direct and vicarious liability

There are two kinds of liability: 'direct' and 'vicarious'. Direct liability is when the employer is *directly* at fault – for example, in failing to employ competent staff or in failing to lay down a safe system of work – and as a result of these failures harm is caused. Vicarious means 'through another', or 'indirect'. The employer can be *indirectly* liable in negligence through the actions of his employees. Vicarious liability is based on the view that an employer should be answerable to the public for harm which his employees have caused, even if the employer himself is entirely without blame.

Read *Speller*, section 5.1.3, pp. 109-110.

To sue the employer, the plaintiff must show the three elements given in *Figure 2*.

1 There was negligence which caused harm and which satisfies the requirements given in *Figure 1*.

2 The person who was negligent was an employee.

3 The employee was acting in the course of employment.

Figure 2: Vicarious liability

Read the following sections of *Speller*:

- Section 5.1.4 'Health authority staff as employees', pp. 110-113

- Section 5.1.2 'The course of employment', pp. 108-109.

Note that even acts prohibited by the employer can be regarded as being performed in the course of employment.

The principles for determining whether an action by an employee is in the course of employment, and therefore that the employer is vicariously liable, are given in *Figure 3*.

> 1 The act is authorised by the employer.

> 2 The act is not authorised but:
> - it is performed for the purposes of the employer's business
> - it is incidental to the employment
> - it is for the protection of the employer's business.

> 3 The act is prohibited by the employer but the prohibition does not take the conduct outside the sphere of employment.

> 4 The employer is under a duty to the person who has suffered loss from the employee's fraud or dishonesty.

Figure 3: Principles for deciding whether an action is in the course of employment

ACTIVITY 4   ALLOW 15 MINUTES

Look at the following list and decide which ones are likely to be defined as activities which are taking place in the course of employment.

1 A cleaner uses the phone for her own private use.

2 A porter helps to evict a trespasser on the ward and the trespasser is seriously injured. The trust employs a security firm for such purposes.

3   A visitor assists in the feeding of a patient who was due to have an operation and therefore NIL BY MOUTH was at the head of her bed.

4   A dietician rushes to help a patient who has fallen out of bed and in trying to lift the patient back onto the bed causes further harm to the patient.

5   A secretary, passing through the ward, is asked to assist in restraining a patient who is mentally disordered. The patient is roughly handled and suffers fractures to his wrists.

6   An ambulance driver on his way back to base after an incident stops off to have a coffee in a cafe and scalds another customer by accident.

7   An ambulance driver on his way back to base after an incident drives through traffic lights and injures three people in another vehicle.

8   The managers expressly forbid the staff to work outside their competence. In an emergency, a theatre nurse acts as first assistant to the surgeon because of the shortage of junior staff and injures the patient with the diathermy.

9   A radiographer is found to be stealing from the clothes of patients left in the changing booths. There is a notice which says that valuables are left at people's own risk.

10 A technician employed by an outside firm wrongly calibrates the radiotherapy equipment. Before the fault is discovered, several patients have an excess dose of radiation. His firm have now gone bankrupt and the patients or their relatives are suing the NHS trust.

11 An agency nurse claims that she is trained to add drugs to intravenous transfusions. However, on the children's ward she fails to calculate the correct dose and a child dies.

Commentary

1   In a court of appeal decision, it was held that a cleaner working for an office cleaning company who had the contract to clean the offices was employed to clean the phones and not to use them. Her employers were therefore held not to be liable for the cost of her overseas calls. She was not acting in the course of employment.

2   Even if the employee was expressly told not to assist in the eviction of trespassers, he was assisting his employers in their enterprise and, therefore, even if he were overzealous, it is probable that his actions would be regarded as being in the course of employment.

3   The visitor is not an employee and therefore the trust would not be liable for the harm caused by her actions. However, there may be negligence by the staff who failed to ensure adequate supervision of the patient (much would depend upon the patient's age and condition), and the employers may therefore be liable for this negligence by their staff.

4   Even though the dietician was doing work not normally associated with dietetics, she was trying to assist the patient who was in difficulties and therefore her actions would probably be regarded as being in the course of employment.

5   Again, the secretary is not employed to restrain patients but she was asked to help and, depending upon the reasonableness of her obeying those instructions, her actions are likely to be seen as being in the course of employment.

6   If he was permitted to have a coffee break and if his employers did not insist that this was taken on trust or health service premises, this could be regarded as being in the course of employment.

7   His return to base is part of his employment even if his driving is negligent. He would be seen as acting in the course of employment.

8   An express prohibition will not necessarily take the action outside the course of employment, so the employers will be vicariously liable in this situation.

9   This theft is not part of the duties of the employer and would not be regarded as being in the course of employment. It may be, however, that there is negligence on the part of other staff if they were aware of her thefts and failed to take appropriate action. The notice ensures that the trust is not considered responsible for the lost property provided it could show it was reasonable to rely upon the notice.

10 This technician was not an employee of the trust which is, therefore, not vicariously liable for his negligence. There may, however, be liability on the part of the trust if one of its employees should have realised the mistake.

11 The agency nurse probably becomes the employee of the trust when taken on and, therefore, the trust would be vicariously liable for her harm. The trust might, however, have an action against the agency itself if it purported to send a nurse who was trained in adding drugs to intravenous transfusions.

Crown indemnity

Doctors and dentists used to be responsible for the payment of compensation for their own negligence. However, since 1 January 1990, the health authorities have accepted responsibility for the liability of all their employees, including doctors and dentists. Circular HC(89)34 set out on pp. 113-116 in section 5.1.5 of *Speller* applies. However, where professional staff work as independent practitioners, such as general practitioners, dentists and pharmacists, or where they have private patients, then they are responsible for their own negligence. You may be interested in reading about the situation that arises in the case of private beds within the NHS (*Speller*, pp. 618-620.)

Court visits

It would be extremely useful for you to visit a court, whether civil or criminal, or to observe an industrial tribunal or professional conduct hearing. There are considerable advantages in going as an observer unconnected with the proceedings so that you can take note of the formalities, procedures, language and the various different persons involved, without being personally caught up in the process. Such an experience would stand you in very good stead should you subsequently have to go to a hearing or even give evidence as part of your job, when there may be insufficient time to go as an observer beforehand.

3: Negligence

Can you remember the four elements in a negligence action? Look back at *Figure 1* to check.

There are two separate stages in an action for compensation for negligence, which are to:

- establish liability

- establish the amount of compensation sought.

This latter task is known as deciding on the *quantum* (Latin for 'how much').

Most actions brought by patients against health authorities and NHS trusts relate to allegations of negligence by the staff of the hospital. Negligence can arise not only in the actions carried out by staff, but from the following failures:

- to communicate with relevant professionals concerned with the patient's care

- to communicate warnings about the treatment to the patient

- to inform the patient about the risks of the treatment before consent is given to the treatment

- to observe the ordinary standards of practice.

The duty of care

All health professionals have a duty of care to their patients, but there may be disputes over the extent of the duty. It would probably not, for example, extend to caring for persons injured in a road accident passed on the way to work, unless, of course, such action was required as part of the contract of employment. The law does not require people to volunteer their services.

There has been some uncertainty over the extent of the duty of care in relation to non-patients. For example, if an informal psychiatric patient leaves the ward contrary to medical advice and injures another person, could the victim hold the hospital liable for those injuries?

Standard of care

Section 6.3.2 of *Speller* explains the standard of care which the courts expect practitioners to follow and what happens when there are different expert views over what action should be taken. It makes it clear that the professional is expected to follow the standard of the reasonable professional who is skilled in a particular art; that where there are different professional views:

> 'it is not sufficient to establish negligence for the plaintiff to show that there is a body of competent professional opinion which considers that the decision was wrong, if there is also a body of professional opinion, equally competent, supporting the decision as having been reasonable in the circumstances.'

(Maynard v Midlands Regional Health Authority, 1984; quoted in *Speller*, p. 164)

Where professionals depart from the accepted practice for good reasons, it is essential that their records state fully what those reasons are. This information is essential to defend their actions or decisions at a later time should harm arise and the plaintiff claim that the professional failed to follow the accepted practice.

Read *Speller,* **section 6.3.2, pp. 155-166,**
up to the heading *'Res ipsa loquitur'.*

The Bolam Test

The Bolam Test states that the law expects the practitioner to practise with the ordinary skill and competence of the type of practitioner to which he belongs. Thus this test has been used not just in the context of medical care, but also for nurses, professionals supplementary to medicine and also professionals outside health care such as accountants, architects, lawyers and others.

ACTIVITY 5   ALLOW **10** MINUTES

Identify one (or more) skill or competency which you perform as part of your professional or managerial duties. Define what you consider is the accepted practice which would not result in harm, such as the procedures you would follow in a particular instance, the information you would give the patient and so on. If you have been able to obtain a copy of any relevant procedures or protocols defining quality of care in your workplace, use them for this activity.

Think about the circumstances in which you might depart from accepted practice. Imagine that harm has occurred as a result of your departure and think what your justification might be. You may like to brainstorm this activity with a group of colleagues.

Commentary

You may have found this activity difficult to tackle, particularly finding a justification for departing from standards of practice. You should be able to appreciate the importance of following the accepted standard of care as, when a plaintiff is alleging negligence, this is central to the defence of the case.

Whilst the courts have to look to national standards of care rather than permit lower local variations to be applied, ultimately they rely upon the evidence of experts to comment on the actions or decisions of the defendants, and in the light of that evidence determine whether the Bolam Test was met. Bear in mind the need to work within accepted practice and therefore to have a definition of what this might be in all aspects of your work.

Res ipsa loquitur: the thing speaks for itself

Read *Speller,* **pp. 166-170.**

Res ipsa loquitur is a legal formula which enables the plaintiff to require the defendant to explain how the events occurred without negligence on the part of the defendant. The plaintiff has to show the following facts:

● something has occurred which would not usually occur if normal precautions were taken

- the events were under the control of the defendant or his employees

- the defendant has not offered any reasonable explanation for what has occurred.

Once the plaintiff has established that *res ipsa loquitur* should be applied, then the defendant has the task of producing an explanation for the events which shows that there was no negligence on his part. It is of particular value to plaintiffs in a situation where they do not have full information as to what took place, such as in an operating theatre. However, it can also arise in other situations which are not clinical. See, for example, the case of *Ward v. Tesco* (1976) given below.

Ward v. Tesco (1976)

On 29 June 1974 at about midday, Mrs Ward went to Tesco supermarket in Liverpool. She walked around the store carrying a wire basket when she felt herself slipping.

> 'She appreciated that she was slipping on something which was sticky. She fell to the ground, and sustained minor injuries. She had not seen what had caused her to slip. It was not suggested, either at the trial or in the Court of Appeal, that she had in any way been negligent in failing to notice what was on the floor as she walked along doing her shopping. When she was picking herself up she appreciated that she had slipped on some pink substance which looked to her like yoghurt. Later, somebody on the defendants' staff found a carton of yoghurt in the vicinity which was two-thirds empty.'
>
> *Ward v. Tesco* (1976)

The defendants arranged for her clothing to be cleaned but she also claimed for personal injuries, which together with costs were agreed at £137.10. The defendants disputed liability. The trial judge found that the plaintiff had made out a *prima facie* case and that the doctrine of *res ipsa loquitur* applied, and he called on the defendants to respond. The Court of Appeal decided by a majority decision (Lord Ormrod dissented) that the plaintiff had made out a case. In the words of Lord Justice Megaw:

> 'It is for the plaintiff to show that there has occurred an event which is unusual and which, in the absence of explanation, is more consistent with fault on the part of the defendants than the absence of fault; and to my mind the learned judge was wholly right in taking that view of the presence of this slippery liquid on the floor of the supermarket in the circumstances of this case: that is that the defendants knew or should have known that it was a not uncommon occurrence; and that if it should happen and should not be promptly attended to, it created a serious risk that customers would fall and injure themselves'.
>
> *Ward v. Tesco* (1976)

This decision was distinguished in a later case which involved spillage in an office block.

ACTIVITY 6   ALLOW **10** MINUTES

Read the article '*Cost of spillage from cup of tea*' (The Times, 1989) which is included as *Resource 2* at the end of this unit and compare it with *Ward v. Tesco* (1976).

How do you think the two situations are different? Would you agree with Lord Justice Ormrod in the Ward case that the doctrine should not apply to that specific situation?

Commentary

In the Ward case, the liability for the safety of floors in a supermarket was the issue being considered. Public access and safety of movement is essential to all parts of the display. In Bell's case, the premises were used as offices to which the public did not have access. Mr Justice Drake said that an office is very different from the situation in a supermarket and he was satisfied that in providing for regular inspections of the building by a competent safety officer, a reasonable system had been established. In contrast, in a supermarket, because of the possibility of frequent spillages by customers, a higher standard of regular inspection would be expected. This was why the doctrine of *res ipsa loquitur* applied in the Tesco case.

Note, however, that even though the doctrine was not applied in Bell's case, the plaintiff succeeded on a balance of probabilities in establishing that there had been negligence by the defendants.

Negligence in communications

ACTIVITY 7   ALLOW 15 MINUTES

Read *Speller*, pp. 173-177, and compare the case of *Chapman v. Rix* with that of *Coles v. Reading and District Hospital Management Committee*.

Make notes on the reasons why in one case there was held to be no negligence and in the other there was.

Look at the potential defendants. Who would you have sued had you been the plaintiff in Chapman's case?

Commentary

In the Chapman case, the House of Lords by a majority found there was no negligence by Dr Rix. It was sufficient for him to have warned the patient to see his own doctor. Note, however, the summary of the two dissenting judges (one of whom was Lord Denning) and the commentary by *Speller* suggesting that if it could be shown subsequently that the common practice was now for the hospital doctor to communicate directly with the patient's GP, then the plaintiff in a subsequent similar case may win.

In Coles' case, the facts were sufficiently dissimilar from Chapman's case to enable the judge to distinguish it from the House of Lords' decision. (If he could not distinguish it, he would have been bound to follow the House of Lords' decision.) The judge found both the hospital and the GP liable in negligence. Had Mr Chapman's widow sued his GP, Dr Mohr, for failure to diagnose the fact that the wound was deep she may have won the case.

> **Read the section entitled 'Failure to communicate warning' in *Speller*, pp. 177-179.**

ACTIVITY 8   ALLOW 15 MINUTES

Tackle either Part 1 or Part 2 of this activity.

Part 1

In your own hospital, get hold of a copy of a leaflet which is given to patients following specific treatments and which advises the patient to watch for certain symptoms or to seek further advice or attention. Examples may include: advice following plastering in the fracture clinic; advice following treatment for a head injury; advice following a sterilisation and the possibility of it not being 100 per cent successful.

Consider how effective the leaflet would be as a defence to a patient if the harm warned about were to arise. Consider also the extent to which staff should take into account the disabilities of the patient or the likelihood of their failing to understand and/or comply with the information given.

Part 2

Read the cases on suicide given in *Speller*, pp. 179 and 180. Make notes for drafting a policy for staff working in all in-patient units on the prevention of suicide by patients. Consider the following questions:

- how would the policy for psychiatric patients be different?

- what should be the standards of care expected of hospitals in relation to preventing patients from self-harm?

- do you consider there is also a duty of care which applies to visitors to protect them from self-harm following bereavement?

Commentary

Whether you looked at the leaflets concerned with warnings to patients or studied a policy to prevent self-harm, you would have needed to have taken into consideration the legal requirements in relation to the duty of care and the need to define what is expected, i.e. the standard of care. Both parts of the activity also required you to take into account the different types of patients and the extent to which they could be relied upon to follow instructions.

The guidelines for staff caring for psychiatric patients would need to provide assistance in carrying out a risk assessment for each individual patient. It would list the criteria used to decide what level of observation each patient should have, and to advise on monitoring and reviewing the risks at regular intervals. The guidance would have to be accompanied by training and the regular assessment of staff. Hospital staff should take into account the following in setting standards for preventing self-harm by patients:

- the seriousness of the risk

- the risk of serious harm

- the practicability of taking precautions

- the objective to be achieved
- what would be reasonable in all the circumstances of the case taking into account cost, time and the patient's situation.

There is no decided case on whether a duty is owed to visitors to prevent them harming themselves following bereavement, but common humanity would suggest that staff should do all that is reasonable in the circumstances to ensure the bereaved are treated kindly and given all the appropriate information and sources of support available to them. Information in written form could be of great assistance but must be carefully drafted.

Delegation and supervision

Read section 6.3.2 of *Speller* from the heading 'Acting reasonably under instruction', pp. 182-188.

This section of *Speller* covers the issues relating to the standard of care which can be expected from different kinds of professions and the different levels within a profession. The basic principle is that the defendant cannot say to a plaintiff: 'Your harm occurred because you were cared for by a junior member of staff. Had you been seen by a senior member of staff you would have been cared for safely'. It is the responsibility of the hospital to ensure that the patient is cared for according to reasonable standards of care. They must ensure the appropriate supervision of junior staff. Note in particular the case of *Wilsher v. Essex Area Health Authority* (1986) on p. 187. The Court of Appeal stated clearly that there was no concept of team liability in law.

If the areas of injuries to unborn children and negligence in relation to abortion and sterilisation are of particular interest to you, read *Speller*, pp. 188-195, sections 6.3.3 and 6.3.4.

Causation

It is not sufficient for the plaintiff to establish a breach of the duty of care in order to obtain compensation. He must also show that it was the breach of the duty of care which caused the harm and that this was reasonably foreseeable, i.e. could have been within the contemplation of the defendant. 'A defendant is not liable for a consequence of a kind which is not foreseeable' is quoted by Lord Wilberforce in *McLoughlin v. O'Brian* 1983. Remember Roe's case (*Speller*, pp. 159-160), for example, where medical knowledge at the time was such that harm was judged not to have been reasonably foreseeable and therefore there was no breach.

Read the case of *Barnett v. Chelsea Hospital Management Committee* on p. 181 of *Speller*.

The facts clearly showed that there was a breach of duty by the casualty officer in failing to examine the patient. The plaintiff lost the case, however, because the patient would have died anyway; i.e. there was no causal link between the failure to examine the patient and the death. The poisoned man would have died even had he been promptly admitted to hospital.

> **Read *Speller*, section 6.3.5, pp. 195-197, where the law relating to causation is set out.**

Harm

The fourth element the plaintiff must establish is harm. Not all harms are recognised by the court as giving rise to compensation in an action for negligence. Thus, for example, damages for nervous shock are only recoverable where the plaintiff was within reasonable proximity to the cause of shock in terms of time and place. Economic loss is only recoverable in tightly defined circumstances. If no harm can be shown, then an action for negligence will not succeed.

Quantum

If the quantum is in dispute between the parties, evidence has to be brought by the plaintiff to show the extent of the pain and suffering and other losses. An example of the various components which make up the quantum is given in *Speller*, p. 199 in the case of Samer Aboul-Hosn. Increasingly the courts have recognised that post-traumatic syndrome is a recognisable disease and can therefore be compensated if the plaintiff can show sufficient proximity to the negligent act of the defendant.

Defences

Many cases are won or lost because of the strength of evidence produced by either side, especially the way in which the witnesses stand up to cross-examination. It is often the facts which are in dispute, and if the plaintiff can show that the facts are as he has pleaded and not as the defendant has described, then the plaintiff wins. Even when the facts are agreed, if the defendant can show that the plaintiff has not established all of the elements shown in *Figure 1*, then the plaintiff will fail to obtain compensation. There are, however, other specific defences which can be pleaded. They are shown in *Figure 4*.

1 Contributory negligence.

2 Voluntary assumption of risk.

3 Limitation of time.

4 Exclusion of liability.

Figure 4: Defences to an action for negligence

Contributory negligence

This may be a partial or complete defence where the defendant can show that the plaintiff failed to take the reasonable care for his own health and safety which could have been expected. Examples from health care might be:

- failure to take the prescribed medication

- failure to follow instructions about lifestyle

- failure of the patient to notify the health professionals about known allergies.

The extent of any reduction of damages because of the patient's contributory negligence will depend upon the capacity and competence of the patient. Thus it would be rare for damages to a child to be reduced because of the child's contributory negligence; See *Speller*, pp. 199-200, section 6.3.7.

Voluntary assumption of risk

The defence of voluntary assumption of risk is unlikely to apply to a patient because, in signing a consent form, he does not take on the risk of the professionals being negligent, although he does take on the risks of unforeseeable accidents occurring which could not reasonably have been prevented. This defence is more likely to apply in sporting events and similar activities.

Limitation of time

'Time runs against the plaintiff' is the legal phrase used to show that legal actions must be brought within a specific time. In actions for personal injuries, time runs from the point that the plaintiff had the knowledge (actual or constructive) that he had suffered harm which could be due to the actions of the defendant. From this point the plaintiff has three years within which to issue the writ. Where the plaintiff is a minor or suffering from mental disorder, time does not commence until the disability ends, i.e. the minor attains 18 years or the mental disorder ends. In addition, the judge has the discretion to disallow the time restraints when it would be just and equitable so to do. See *Speller*, pp. 125-134, section 5.2.

Exclusion of liability

Liability for negligence which results in personal injury or death cannot be excluded by the defendant whether by notice or contract. This is the effect of the Unfair Contract Terms Act 1977. However, where the negligence has led to loss or damage to property, then liability can be excluded if it is reasonable for the defendant to rely upon the exclusion. It is the responsibility of the defendant to show the reasonableness of relying upon the exclusion notice or clause.

Procedure in the civil courts

The stages that would be followed in an action in the civil courts, specifically in the High Court, are given below. County courts can now hear cases where up to £50,000 is being claimed. The procedure should be simpler and faster in the county courts.

1 Writ issued.

2 Writ is served (within four months of issue).

3 Statement of claim is provided.

4 Defence is issued.

5 Further and better particulars of each may be requested.

6 Discovery of documents.

7 Interrogatories.

8 Pre-trial review.

9 Hearing.

During a number of these stages, various documents – known as pleadings, which are usually drafted by barristers – are exchanged between the parties and this can take many years.

Summary

- Health professionals are accountable under the civil, criminal and employment law and through their professional registration.

- An action for negligence must show that there is a duty of care, that there has been a breach in the duty of care and that this has resulted in reasonably foreseeable harm.

- The employer can be indirectly liable in negligence through the actions of his employees.

- The Bolam Test states that the law expects the practitioner to practise with the ordinary skill and competence of the type of practitioner to which he belongs.

Before you move on to Session Two, check that you have achieved the objectives given at the beginning of this session and, if not, review the appropriate sections.

SESSION TWO

Employment law

Introduction

The establishment of NHS trusts and the decentralisation of the determination of contractual conditions for certain groups of staff has meant that major changes can take place within the NHS. This could result in the eventual disappearance of the distinctions which currently exist in the framework for contractual conditions for NHS and non-NHS staff. At present, most NHS trusts are still adhering to the Whitley Council conditions (conditions agreed and set nationally through a system of collective bargaining) for their staff. However, this may change in the future. This session will consider the arena of employment contracts and the relationship between employee and employer.

Chapter 17 of *Speller* deals more extensively with employment law and in greater detail than this unit, and can therefore be referred to if you have a particular interest in this area.

In this session we will be looking at:

- the terms and conditions of the contract of employment
- statutory provisions relating to employment
- disciplinary and grievance procedures
- redundancy
- trade union rights and obligations.

Session objectives

When you have completed this session, you should be able to:

- explain the basic concepts which apply to the relationship of employer and employee
- describe the elements within a contract of employment and its place within the context of the statutory regulations
- outline the changing scene of collective bargaining: the Whitley Council system and the possibilities of local negotiations with the establishment of NHS trusts.

1: The employer–employee relationship

Master and servant: employer and employee

Many old cases refer to the terms 'master' and 'servant' – once the customary way of referring to an employer and his employees. *Speller* (sections 17.1.2-17.1.7) defines what is meant by an employee, and distinguishes an employer's relationship with his employee from other relationships, such as with an independent contractor, a trainee and so on. The difference between an employee and an independent contractor is important in the law of tort, as we saw in the discussion on accountability in Session One, since the employer is vicariously liable for the negligence of his employee whilst the latter is working in the course of employment. He is not (except in very limited circumstances) liable for the negligence of an independent contractor. Thus, an NHS trust is liable for the negligence of a consultant, whether full-time or part-time, working on trust business; a family health services authority, however, is not liable for the negligence of one of its independent contractors, such as a general practitioner. The distinction is also important in the field of employment law since an independent contractor or self-employed person is not entitled to the statutory benefits given to employees under employment legislation.

The employee is said to have a **contract of employment** or **service**; the independent contractor has a **contract for services**.

Read *Speller*, **sections 17.1.1-17.1.7, pp. 417-422.**

The contract of employment

This lies at the heart of the relationship between employer and employee. It may not be evidenced in writing but it creates a legal relationship between employee and employer which can only be ended in specific ways and gives rights and duties to both parties.

There are various sources of the terms that make up a contract of employment:

- express terms agreed between the parties

- express terms laid down through collective bargaining which are incorporated into the contract

- express terms as under the previous point, but which are agreed subsequent to the contract of employment coming into being

- implied terms which are implied by the law as being part of the contract – some are set down in common law, some imposed by statutes

- statutory rights and obligations set out in legislation.

Express and implied terms

Express terms are those that have been explicitly drawn up as part of the contract, either by the parties themselves or through the mechanism of collective bargaining. For example, the title of the post and the starting date will be agreed by the parties; the salary, the holidays, sick pay and pension may already have been agreed through collective bargaining.

Implied terms are those terms which the law imputes to a contract and which are part of the legally enforceable obligations, even though the parties might never have referred to them. Examples of implied terms are:

- the employer should take all reasonable care for the health and safety of the employee

- the employer should treat the employee with respect and trust

- the employer should not prevent the employee from performing his contract of employment

- the employee will act with all reasonable care and skill

- the employee will obey the reasonable orders of the employer.

Common law and statutes

Much of the law relating to employment derives from the decision by judges in different cases which, as we discussed in Session One, is known as 'common law'. However, there are also a considerable number of Acts of Parliament which relate to the employer–employee relationship. One of the most important is the Employment Protection (Consolidation) Act 1978, which brought together a number of previous statutes. The 1978 Act has in its turn been amended by subsequent legislation which we will be looking at in this session.

Wrongful and unfair dismissal

Wrongful dismissal is a dismissal contrary to the contract of employment. Thus, if a contract stipulates that the employee should be given two months' notice and the employee who is not in breach of contract is only given one month's notice, that would constitute a wrongful dismissal.

Unfair dismissal is a creation of statute. It was designed to give protection to those employees who had worked faithfully for an employer for at least a specified time (currently two years for those working at least 16 hours a week, or five years for those working at least eight hours) and then were dismissed by being given the specified period of notice. Such employees had no remedy in the county courts for breach of contract, since the employer had acted within the contract of employment. It was, however, seen to be a grossly unfair situation. Hence the concept of unfair dismissal was introduced by statute and provisions laid down as to when a dismissal was fair and the remedies which were available to the employee if it was unfair.

> **Read** *Speller*, **section 17.1.9, pp. 424-432, which covers the law relating to work rules, the written particulars of employment, time off work and the termination of the contract of employment.**

ACTIVITY 9   ALLOW 15 MINUTES

You were asked to obtain a copy of your contract of employment for this activity. If you do not have a contract in writing, ask the personnel department to provide you with a statement of the written particulars. It is sufficient to comply with the law for the employer to refer the employee to a document to which the employee has access which covers those particulars, such as the *Whitley Council Handbook*. If applicable to you, check out the general conditions of work and also the specific conditions which relate to your profession and grade in the *Whitley Council Handbook*. Compare your conditions of work with the specific terms listed in *Speller*, pp. 425-426, and make sure you know your position in each of the areas covered.

Commentary

After completing this activity you should have a better understanding of your contractual position and, if relevant to your job, you may be aware of the Whitley Council regulations which relate to your profession and grade. Remember that any statement of written particulars drawn up under the statutory duty is not a contract, but may be evidence of what the terms of the contract are.

Other terms which are part of the contract of employment

The contract of employment also contains terms which are the result of legislation, i.e. statutory rights given to the employee. These cover:

- time off work for various activities

- the right not to be dismissed on grounds of pregnancy

- the right to return to work after pregnancy

- other rights relating to the pregnant employee

- the right not to be unfairly dismissed.

2: Unfair dismissal

Speller section 17.2 sets out:

- the rules and principles relating to unfair dismissal

- what is meant by constructive dismissal

- the reasons for fair dismissal recognised by statute

- situations where a dismissal would be automatically unfair

- the remedies for unfair dismissal

- the continuity of employment when employees are transferred to an NHS trust.

Skim read section 17.2, pp. 432-451, of *Speller*, making brief notes on the main points.

ACTIVITY 10   ALLOW 60 MINUTES

Maria Price had worked as a staff nurse for seven years with Roger Park District Health Authority on the intensive care ward. In 1993 an application was accepted for Roger Park to become an NHS trust, and this was established in April 1994. All staff were assured continuity of service. Maria was an active union member and started to complain that, under the trust, staffing levels on intensive care had been cut to the extent that patients were in danger. She put her concerns in writing and had a confrontational meeting with her manager who warned her that if she continued to act with such disloyalty to the trust she would be dismissed. Maria stated that if that was the attitude of the management, she did not want to work for such an outfit. To this the manager responded in the temper of the moment, 'then that will suit all of us'.

Maria was subsequently advised by a union official that by acting in that way the manager, and therefore the trust, was acting in fundamental breach of its contract with her and therefore it was considered that she had the right to see the contract as ended by breach of contract by her employers. She therefore left work but made an application to the Industrial Tribunal claiming that she had been constructively dismissed. Subsequently, the trust put in a defence to her application raising the following grounds:

- she resigned her job and therefore there was no dismissal

- if it is held that there was a dismissal, then it was justified on the basis of her conduct since she failed to take the appropriate steps to make her grievances known.

With a group of colleagues, play out this situation with some of you representing the employee and some the employer. Take it in turns to put forward the respective arguments. Make a list of evidence which each party would require to place before any hearing and the kinds of witnesses who might be summoned.

If you are unable to get a group together, analyse the strengths and weaknesses of each side in this dispute yourself and list the evidence and witnesses who would be needed. Decide who you think should win and give the reasons for that decision.

Look at the copy of the disciplinary procedure for your own workplace you have been asked to obtain and decide if the employers followed this in the way that Maria was dealt with.

Commentary

Whether on your own or with colleagues you will need to decide what documentary evidence is required by both parties. This is considered below. Note also the changes introduced by the Employment Act 1980 in relation to the test of reasonableness and the burden of proof given in *Speller*, p. 436. Whether the employer acted reasonably often depends on the extent to which the employer followed the disciplinary procedure in dealing with the employee.

Documentary evidence required at an industrial tribunal hearing in a case such as Maria's would probably include the following. For the employer:

- the contract of employment with the employee

- the code of practice relating to disciplinary procedures

- any trust policy relating to whistle-blowing and freedom of speech as well as any government circulars and national guidance on the topic

- any correspondence with the employee.

The employee may wish to produce any of the above documents and also:

- her own correspondence

- the code of professional conduct and other guidance from professional registration bodies

- guidelines on staffing in intensive care units.

Witnesses might include:

- the manager of the intensive care unit

- other employees in intensive care

- the trust personnel manager

- the director responsible for intensive care

- any others who could give evidence on the dispute.

Maria would need to fulfil the four requirements given in *Speller*, section 17.2.2, in order to establish that the circumstances were appropriate for her to terminate the contract without notice by reason of her employer's conduct. Many of these are factual issues relating to what the employee did, how she conveyed her decision to the employers and when she took the decision to leave. If it can be established that there was a causal connection between the employer's conduct and the employee's leaving, and also that the conduct would justify her in so doing, the dismissal could be regarded as not fair. Maria could argue that the trust broke its contract by not maintaining adequate staffing levels. The manager's behaviour in the office would also be taken into account in determining the reasonableness of the employer in treating the employee's conduct as justifying dismissal. The manager clearly showed that he was not prepared to listen to Maria's concerns and warnings. Note, however, that the conduct of the employee is potentially a fair reason for dismissal (see *Speller*, pp. 435-438, sections 17.2.3 and 17.2.4).

More tolerance would be expected of a larger employer with more resources where one individual's misconduct is likely to have less impact on the organisation than would be the case for a small employer.

ACTIVITY 11   ALLOW 30 MINUTES

You were asked to obtain material from your employer and the Department of Employment relating to employment practices for this activity. See whether the terms in your contract of employment are better than those laid down by statute. If the reverse is true, you should be able to claim the more beneficial rights given by statute.

Included amongst the information you collect there should be policies relating to discrimination on the grounds of sex or race. If you have a particular interest in this area of employment law, see *Speller*, pp. 451-459, section 17.3.

Examine the documents you have obtained from your employer and address the following questions:

- to what extent is the implementation of these policies monitored in your workplace?

- is there an officer responsible for some or all of the policies?

- how often are they reviewed?

- are there any noticeable gaps in the employment policies which your employer has produced?

- is there a policy relating to disabled employees?

- are there policies relating to training opportunities?

- do staff have a right to insist on attending training sessions?

Commentary

The difference between direct and indirect discrimination is important. Note that there is no statutory provision prohibiting discrimination against disabled persons. An attempt has been made to introduce legislation to give legal rights to disabled people in relation to employment, but so far this has failed. Employers employing more than 250 people are required to employ three per cent of their workforce from those registered as disabled, but apart from that there is no right of a disabled person to complain through the courts that there has been discrimination against him because of his disability.

This activity has been concerned with the practical preparation and implementation of employment policies in the workplace. As a result of undertaking this activity, you should be aware of any gaps within your own organisation in relation to either the existence or the implementation of employment policies.

3: Redundancy

It is likely that the changes taking place in the health services will lead to more staff being made redundant, and it is essential that staff and managers are acquainted with the law relating to redundancy.

Speller contains two sections concerned with redundancy: the first covers the statutory provisions, the second the particular scheme which operates in the NHS. This scheme defines suitable alternative work in a very comprehensive way so that if a post is offered to a person facing redundancy it might be very difficult to establish that it is reasonable to refuse that post.

> **Read sections 17.4 (pp. 459-461), 17.5.3 (pp. 464-467) and 17.13 (pp. 507-514) of** *Speller.*

ACTIVITY 12   ALLOW 30 MINUTES

Obtain a copy of your employer's policy on redundancy. It may be that he has declared that there will be no redundancies, in which case obtain a copy of this declaration. With reference to this and the sections of *Speller* you have just read, tackle the following questions:

1   What procedure must be followed before a person is made redundant?

2   What kind of work would be regarded as suitable alternative work?

3   How can an employee challenge a redundancy decision?

4 How is compensation calculated for an employee being made redundant?

5 Could an employer pay more than the statutory defined amounts?

6 If an employee accepted a redundancy offer, could he then claim that he has been unfairly dismissed?

7 In preparing policies for the management of change for your employer, what would you include in relation to redundancy policy and practice?

Commentary

By referring to *Speller* and your employer's redundancy policy you should be able to answer these questions.

4: Trade union rights and obligations

Trade union powers have gradually been diluted over the last 20 years. Their control over their members, their earlier right to insist on a closed shop where the employer would only employ members of their own union, the right to go on strike, the right of a person to support others on strike where that person is not part of the dispute, their collection of moneys and the control of their funds have all been subject to legislation.

ACTIVITY 13   ALLOW 45 MINUTES

Hopefully you have been able to obtain from the local steward for the trade union applicable to you a copy of the details of the constitution, function, membership rules and services provided for members. Read this and note in particular any role that the union has in relation to collective bargaining at local level for its members. To what extent do you consider that the trade union can have an important part to play in industrial and employment relations at local level?

You were also asked to get hold of two booklets on employment legislation produced by the Employment Department: *Industrial Action and the Law* (PL 943) and *Union Membership and Non-Membership Rights* (PL 871 (REV3)). These take account of the legislation up to and including the Trade Union Reform and Employment Rights Act 1993. Read all of the first and Part II of the second. Are there any terms in your contract of employment about strikes or trade union membership? How far does your contract support what you have read in the booklets?

Commentary

Answers to this activity are likely to vary considerably, as some trust boards make greater use than others of the role which local shop stewards can play. Note the statutory rights which trade union officers and members still enjoy and the fact that a dismissal in connection with trade union activities would entitle the employee to challenge that dismissal in the industrial tribunal without showing the continuous employment service which is required to be shown in other circumstances.

5: Future developments

NHS trusts have the power to agree the terms of the contract of employment for their staff through local collective bargaining. A contract of employment cannot be changed without the consent of both parties, but new contracts can be offered to new employees and as a condition of promotion. You should be alert to local changes introduced by your employer and to the procedures for local bargaining.

Summary

- There is a contract of employment between every employer and employee whether or not it is written down.

- As well as there being express terms in a contract of employment, there are implied terms which are legally enforceable obligations understood by the law to be present, whether or not formally agreed between the parties.

- Employees have statutory protection from unfair dismissal if they have been continuously in the employ of the employer for the requisite length of time.

- Although the power of trade unions has been diminished over the last 20 years, there are still statutory rights for trade union officers and members, including the right not to be dismissed for engaging in trade union activities.

Before you move on to Session Three, check that you have achieved the objectives given at the beginning of this session and, if not, review the appropriate sections.

SESSION THREE

Health and safety laws

Introduction

The aim of this session is to explore the laws relating to health and safety in the workplace and to give you the opportunity to undertake practical work in the application of health and safety regulations to your working environment.

Speller, chapters 9 and 20, cover the areas we will be looking at and you will be asked to read specific sections as you work through this session. Also relevant to health and safety are professional accountability and employment law, which we discussed in the first two sessions.

Session objectives

When you have completed this session you should be able to:

- summarise the legal framework of health and safety in the workplace

- give an account of the health and safety responsibilities of the employer and the employee

- implement the health and safety regulations in your workplace

- carry out a risk assessment

- discuss the powers of the Health and Safety Inspectorate and the enforcement provisions for health and safety in the health services.

1: The legal framework for health and safety in the workplace

Figure 5 lists the laws relating to health and safety in the workplace, some of which we will be considering in this session.

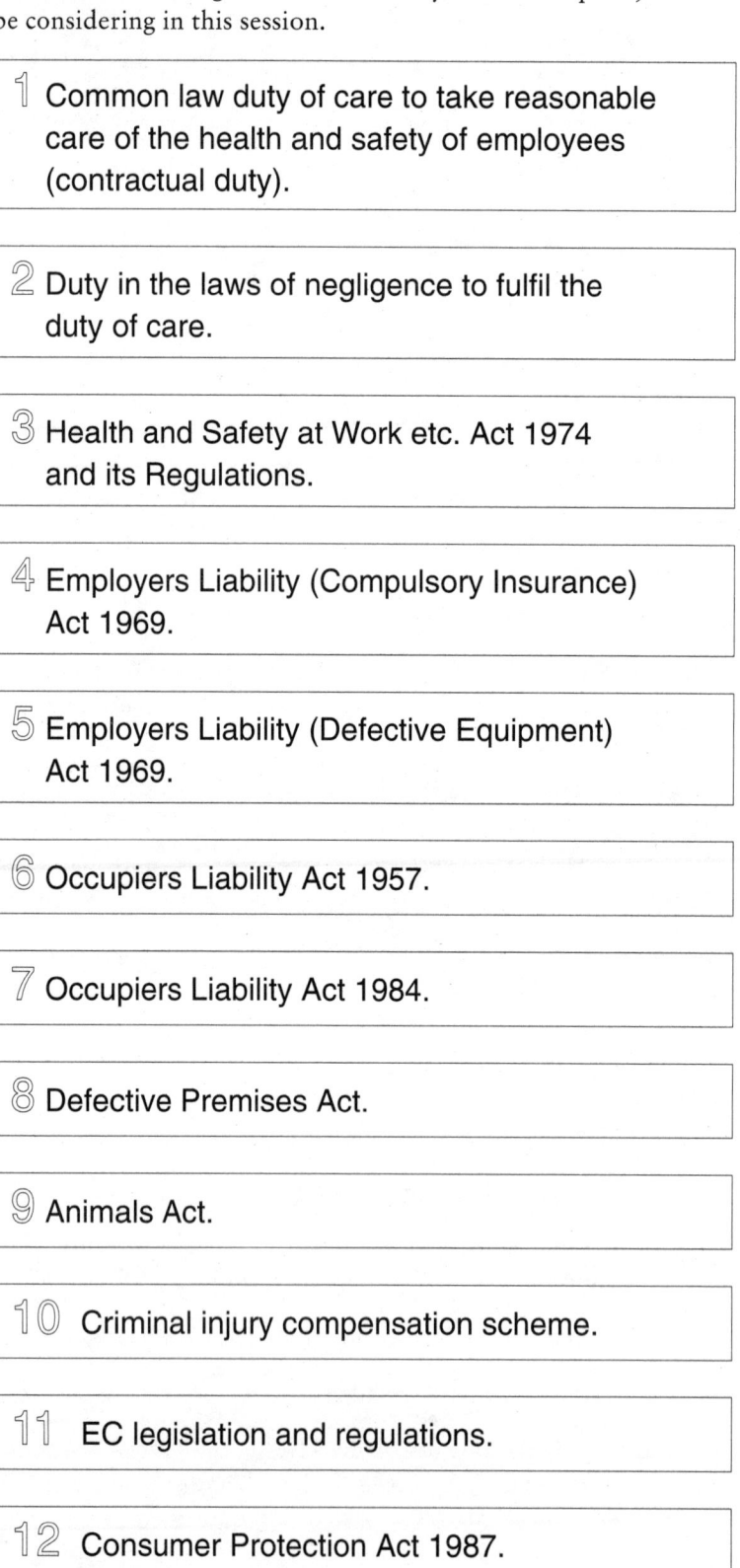

1 Common law duty of care to take reasonable care of the health and safety of employees (contractual duty).

2 Duty in the laws of negligence to fulfil the duty of care.

3 Health and Safety at Work etc. Act 1974 and its Regulations.

4 Employers Liability (Compulsory Insurance) Act 1969.

5 Employers Liability (Defective Equipment) Act 1969.

6 Occupiers Liability Act 1957.

7 Occupiers Liability Act 1984.

8 Defective Premises Act.

9 Animals Act.

10 Criminal injury compensation scheme.

11 EC legislation and regulations.

12 Consumer Protection Act 1987.

13 Fire precautions regulations.

Figure 5: Laws relating to the health and safety of the employee

Read *Speller*, section 20.8.4, pp. 584-588.

The Health and Safety at Work etc. Act 1974 sets out the principal provisions covering the criminal laws on health and safety. The Act is based on the Robens Report (Committee on Health and Safety at Work, 1972), which recommended the co-operation of employers and employees as the basic foundation of a firm health and safety policy. Safety committees and safety representatives were suggested as the mechanism of ensuring that health and safety concerns were brought to the attention of the management. Regulations (SI 1977 No. 500) relating to the appointment of safety representatives by safety committees were brought into force in 1978. Regulation 3 states that:

'   . . . a recognised trade union may appoint safety representatives from amongst the employees in all cases where one or more employees are employed by an employer by whom it is recognised . . .

(2)   Where the employer has been notified in writing . . . each such safety representative shall have the functions set out in Regulation 4 below.'

Regulation 3 (3) covers the situation when a person ceases to be a safety representative due to the trade union ending the appointment, the person concerned leaving the workplace or resigning. The relevant parts of Regulation 4 are quoted below:

'(4)   A person appointed . . . as a safety representative shall so far as is reasonably practicable either have been employed by his employer throughout the preceding two years or have had at least two years' experience in similar employment.

4 (1) In addition to his function under section 2(4) of the 1974 Act to represent the employees in consultation with the employer under section 2(6) of the 1974 Act . . . each safety representative shall have the following functions:

(a) to investigate potential hazards and dangerous occurrences at the workplace (whether or not they are drawn to his attention by the employees he represents) and to examine the causes of accident at the workplace;

(b) to investigate complaints by any employee he represents relating to that employee's health, safety or welfare at work;

(c) to make representations to the employer on matters arising out of sub-paragraphs (a) and (b) above;

(d) to make representations to the employer on general matters affecting the health, safety or welfare at work of the employees at the workplace;

(e) to carry out inspections . . .

(f) to represent the employees he was appointed to represent in consultations at the workplace with inspectors of the Health and Safety Executive and of any other enforcing authority;

(g) to receive information from inspectors in accordance with section 28(8) of the 1974 Act; and

(h) to attend meetings of safety committees . . . but . . . no function

45

given to a safety representative by this paragraph shall be construed as imposing any duty on him.'

Regulation 4(2) gives the safety representative the right to take such time off with pay during the employee's working hours as are necessary for the purposes of carrying out the defined functions and undergoing the necessary training.

Regulation 5 covers the inspection of the workplace.

Regulation 6 covers inspections following notifiable accidents, occurrences and diseases.

Regulation 7 covers the inspection of documents and provision of information.

Regulation 8 covers cases where safety representatives need not be employees.

Regulation 9 covers the appointment of safety committees.

Regulation 10 gives to the Health and Safety Commission (HSC) the power to grant exemptions from these Regulations.

Regulation 11 provides for the safety representative to apply to an industrial tribunal if he has not been permitted to take paid time off in accordance with these Regulations.

The Health and Safety at Work Act 1974 sets out clearly the duties placed upon the employer. The general duty under section 2(1) is given in *Speller*, p. 584, the specific duties under subsection 2(2) are given in *Resource 3* at the back of this unit. Take the time now to read *Resource 3* and note in particular the opening words of point 2. The intention is that the examples of duties given in subsections 2a to 2e should not limit or diminish the responsibilities of the employer.

Section 7 of the Act places a statutory duty on the employee:

'It shall be the duty of every employee while at work:

1   to take reasonable care for the health and safety of himself and of others who may be affected by his acts or omissions at work; and

2   as regards any duty or requirement imposed on his employer or any other person . . . to co-operate with him so far as is reasonable to enable that duty to be performed or complied with.'

In addition, Section 8 makes it an offence to tamper with any health and safety provision:

'no person shall intentionally or recklessly interfere with or misuse anything provided in the interest of health, safety or welfare in pursuance of any relevant statutory provisions.'

Supplementary to the provisions of the Act there are numerous regulations covering specific aspects of health and safety. In order to comply with EC directives, the following new regulations came into force on 1 January 1993:

● The Provision and Use of Work Equipment Regulations (SI 1992 No. 2932)

● The Manual Handling Operations Regulations (SI 1992 No. 2793)

● The Workplace (Health, Safety and Welfare) Regulations (SI 1992 No. 3004)

● The Personal Protective Equipment at Work Regulations (SI 1992 No. 2966)

- Health and Safety (Display Screen Equipment) Regulations (SI 1992 No. 2792)

- Management of Health and Safety in the Workplace Regulations (SI 1992 No. 2051).

ACTIVITY 14   ALLOW **90** MINUTES

From the list of the above Regulations, select one which is likely to be most relevant to the work you do, but do not choose the management of health and safety at work as this will be discussed in the next section of this session.

In the Introduction to the unit you were asked to write to your local office of the Health and Safety Executive (HSE) to obtain material on health and safety. If you haven't already done so, get hold of the HSE booklet that covers the particular area you have selected from the above list; you may be able to get hold of a copy from your unit manager or a health and safety officer at your workplace. Spend some time studying it and then work out a strategy for implementing the regulations in your workplace.

Commentary

Once you have received the pack from the HSE you should be able to ensure that you continue to receive advice about new publications so that you keep abreast with developments in health and safety. It might be worth finding out if there is an HMSO retail outlet near you so that you can visit the shop and obtain the publications.

You may have found this activity time-consuming and perhaps you found that you were frequently asking yourself basic questions to which you did not know the answer. It is a good idea to find out (if you don't already know) who your safety representative is and who chairs the safety committee. You can then ask them any questions you have or take up any concerns with them directly.

2: Management of Health and Safety at Work Regulations

The Regulations relating to the management of health and safety in the workplace cover the areas shown below:

- risk assessment

- health and safety arrangements

- health surveillance

- health and safety assistance

- danger

- information

- co-operation and co-ordination

- self-employment

- training

- employer's duties

- different workers

- exemption certificates

- exclusion of civil liability.

Risk assessment

The Regulations place the need to assess the risk of hazards at the heart of the management of health and safety in the workplace. They require the following steps to be taken by the employer:

1   Assessment

- familiarisation with the relevant literature

- the identification of risks to the health and safety of employees and to the health and safety of persons not in his employment

- the suitable and sufficient assessment of risk

- the identification and prioritisation of the measures required

- ensuring that the measures are relevant, effective and valid for some time ahead.

2   Review

- when assessment is no longer valid

- in the event of significant change.

3   Recording

- of significant findings

- of employees especially at risk.

4   Prevention and protection

- if possible, avoid risk altogether

- combat risks at source

- adapt work to the individual

- use technological and technical progress

- risk management as part of a coherent policy and approach

- give priority to measures which protect all

- ensure workers understand what they must do

- ensure existence of an active health and safety culture.

Note the key stages in the assessment of risk are:

1 assessment

2 review

3 recording

4 preventative and protective measures.

This is useful to bear in mind when applying health and safety regulations in other contexts.

One important feature of this assessment of risk is the emphasis on real rather than imaginary risks. The guidance on the Regulations states: 'Trivial risks can usually be ignored as can risks arising from routine activities associated with life in general . . . or should be unless there is evidence of significant relevance to the particular work activity' (HSC, 1992, p. 3, para. 9).

The emphasis is also on co-operation across the workforce incorporating both managers and employees. The creation of a 'health and safety culture' is seen as an objective. Training, the assessment of the capabilities of employees and the promotion of involvement by employees in health and safety analysis and measures is vital.

Training

'Every employer shall, in entrusting tasks to his employees, take into account their capabilities as regards health and safety.
Every employer shall ensure that his employees are provided with adequate health and safety training'

Regulation 11

The Regulations go on to identify the circumstances when training should be given, such as on recruitment and on exposure to new and increased risks due to:

● the transfer or change of responsibilities

● the introduction of new work equipment or a change respecting work equipment

● the introduction of new technology

● the introduction of a new system of work, or a change respecting a system of work.

The Regulations go on to specify that:

'Training shall:

1. Be repeated periodically where appropriate.

2. Be adapted to take account of any new or changed risks to health and safety.

3. Take place during working hours.'

Regulation 11(3)

These Regulations place a clear responsibility upon the employer to fund training for the employee at clearly specified times. The trained employee can more effectively fulfil his functions under the Health and Safety at Work Act and

Regulations. These duties are specified below:

'Every employee shall use equipment etc. in accordance with training and instructions.

Every employee shall inform his employer:

1   of any work situation which would . . . reasonably represent a serious and immediate danger to health and safety, and

2   any matter which would . . . [represent] a shortcoming in the employer's protection arrangements.'

You can see that the Regulations place clear duties not only upon employers but also upon each individual employee.

3: The Control of Substances Hazardous to Health Regulations

Assessment and action

The Control of Substances Hazardous to Health Regulations (COSHH) (SI 1988 No. 1657) require employers to manage the risk relating to the health of employees as a result of the use of substances hazardous to health. The first step required is an assessment of the risk, the second the decision as to what is the appropriate action as a result of that assessment. Reference should be made to the many publications to be obtained from HMSO prepared by the Health and Safety Commission or Executive.

ACTIVITY 15   ALLOW 45 MINUTES

Read the COSHH Regulations which can be obtained from HMSO.

Identify any substances used in your workplace which are hazardous. In the light of the COSHH Regulations, make an assessment as to the risk and list the actions which should be taken to remove or minimise the risk.

Commentary

Did you find that you were using a similar process to the one we looked at in the section about risk assessment: assessment; review; recording; prevention and protection?

A COSHH assessment can be carried out in a wide variety of workplaces: an office, a ward, a clinic, a department of any kind. It is almost impossible to find premises where COSHH substances would not be present.

On-going procedures

Once you have done your initial assessment and determined what preventative or protective measures you must take, it is important to establish the dates or the circumstances when the exercise should be repeated, and to set up a system to ensure that this actually occurs.

4: Enforcement provisions

The Health and Safety Inspectorate

The important point about the statutory duties set down in the statutes and the regulations on health and safety is that ultimately they can be enforced through the criminal laws. The Health and Safety Inspectorate can bring prosecutions and they have many other powers which are based on the fact that to resist the Inspectorate in the carrying out of these statutory powers is an offence. Amongst their powers are:

- the prohibition notice (S.22)

- the improvement notice (S.21).

A prohibition notice can be served where the inspector fears the activities may involve a risk of serious injury. It has the effect of preventing the carrying on of the activities until the law is complied with. An improvement notice requires a person to take specified remedial steps within a specified time.

Other powers of the Health and Safety Inspectorate are set out in Section 20 of the Health and Safety at Work Act 1974, which is included as *Resource 4* at the end of this unit. Read this through now.

Read *Speller*, section 20.1, pp. 550-553.

Immunity from prosecution

Until the implementation of the NHS (Amendment) Act 1986, health authorities enjoyed immunity from prosecution and from prohibition and enforcement notices on the grounds that 'the crown does not prosecute the crown'. However, following the Stanley Royd food poisoning, legislation was passed to remove this immunity from the enforcement provisions of the health and safety legislation and the food legislation so that health authorities are no longer crown bodies for the purposes of this legislation. The NHS and Community Care Act 1990 removed further immunity and, apart from specific exemptions listed in the 1990 Act, health authorities are liable to the full effect of health and safety and other legislation. Some immunities in relation to other legislation remain. The following Acts are those listed in schedule 8 of the NHS and Community Care Act 1990 from which the health authorities are exempt:

- Employers' Liability (Compulsory Insurance) Act 1969 (see *Speller*, pp. 562-563)

- Vehicles (Excise) Act 1971 – road tax not payable (see *Speller*, p. 52)

- Copyright, Designs and Patents Act 1988

- Road Traffic Act 1988 – third-party insurance cover (see *Speller*, pp. 52-53).

It is now possible not only for the individual employee to be prosecuted under health and safety legislation, but also for the health service employer to be prosecuted, whether a district health authority or an NHS trust.

Civil liability

The duty of care which we discussed in Session One also applies in health and safety. You may remember the elements that need to be shown in an action for negligence which were given in *Figure 1*. If these can be shown to exist, then compensation may be payable to someone who has suffered harm. In addition, it is possible to claim compensation through the criminal injury compensation scheme. This obviates the necessity to claim through the civil courts and is important if there are no funds from which the plaintiff in a civil suit can claim.

Professional accountability

In Session One we looked at professional codes of conduct and how they can be used to determine the standard of professional conduct. They can also have a bearing on health and safety. In the case of nurses, midwives and health visitors, many of the clauses of the UKCC's code of conduct relate to the health and safety of patients, colleagues and the general public.

'1   act always in such manner as to promote and safeguard the interests and well-being of patients and clients;

2   ensure that no action or omission on your part, or within your sphere of responsibility, is detrimental to the interests, condition or safety of patients and clients;

3   maintain and improve your professional knowledge and competence;

4   acknowledge any limitations in your knowledge and competence and decline any duties or responsibilities unless able to perform them in a safe and skilled manner;'

'11   report to an appropriate person or authority, having regard to the physical, psychological and social effects on patients and clients, any circumstances in the environment of care which could jeopardise standards of practice;

12   report to an appropriate person or authority any circumstances in which safe and appropriate care for patients and clients cannot be provided;

13   report to an appropriate person or authority where it appears that the health or safety of colleagues is at risk, as such circumstances may compromise standards of practice and care;

14   assist professional colleagues, in the context of your own knowledge, experience and sphere of responsibility, to develop their professional competence, and assist others in the care team, including informal carers, to contribute safely and to a degree appropriate to their roles'.

(UKCC, 1992)

ACTIVITY 16   ALLOW **10** MINUTES

Apply any of the above clauses from the UKCC's code of conduct to your own work situation, and measure the extent to which your own work practices comply with these professional requirements.

Commentary

If you obtain sight of any reported cases of misconduct from the UKCC you will see that many of them relate to health and safety. If misconduct is established it can lead to striking off or suspension from the register, a postponement of a decision, a caution, a referral to the health committee or no action being taken.

5: Contractual duties

> **Read *Speller*, sections 20.2 and 20.3, pp. 553-561, which set out the responsibilities of the employer to the employee under the contract of employment, in addition to those in section 20.1 which you have already read.**

Each employee has a contract of employment with his employer which requires the employee to abide by the express terms given in the contract. In addition, there are implied terms binding on the employee and employer which are shown below. The employee must:

- obey the reasonable instructions of the employer

- act with all reasonable care and skill in the performance of his duties.

The employer must:

- take all reasonable care for the employee's safety in:

    - employing competent staff

    - ensuring a safe system of work

    - providing safe plant, premises and equipment.

Failure to fulfil the contract on the employer's part could lead to an action for negligence if harm occurs; there is also the possibility of an action by an employee for constructive dismissal or breach of contract.

Failure to fulfil the contract on the employee's part could lead to disciplinary proceedings and, in cases of gross misconduct, dismissal.

ACTIVITY 17 — ALLOW 15 MINUTES

Look through your contract of employment. Are there any express terms which deal with the issue of health and safety? If so, analyse the extent to which you are following them. If not, look at the implied terms set out above and consider how you would draft express terms to cover these requirements.

Commentary

All employees have both a statutory duty and a contractual duty to take reasonable care for the health and safety of themselves and others. In addition, those employees who are professionally registered also have a duty under a code of professional conduct to take precautions to maintain standards of health and safety. This activity should show the link between these duties and emphasise the personal responsibility of each employee in relation to health and safety.

6: Liability under the law

Liability for premises

> **Read *Speller*, Chapter 9, pp. 316-331. This section discusses the provisions of the two Occupier's Liability Acts of 1957 and 1984; the first covers the duty towards visitors on site, the second the duty towards trespassers.**

Note the difficulties which community staff would have in claiming compensation for injuries which have resulted from defective premises or furnishings and fittings. Unless their employer is the occupier or owner of the premises on which the injuries occurred, he would not be responsible and they would have to seek compensation from others.

ACTIVITY 18   ALLOW 10 MINUTES

An NHS trust contracts with a firm of painters and decorators for a ward to be redecorated. Because of the pressure on beds it has not been possible to empty the ward before work commenced, and the painters had to decorate whilst other activities were taking place. They were painting the corridor ceiling and placed notices warning people of the dangers. Unfortunately, a patient bumped into the ladder and fell, causing further harm to his broken hand. He is claiming compensation. Consider the following questions:

- what advice would you give him?

- how would your answer differ if the injured person was a child of 8 years?

- would your advice be different if the injured person was a trespasser?

Commentary

The possible defendants would be the NHS trust and the firm of painters, since both are occupiers of the premises. The former would try to rely upon 2(4)(b) of the Occupiers Liabilty Act 1957, in that it was reasonable for them to use independent contractors for the work and that they had satisfied themselves that the contractor was competent and the work was properly done. The contractor might try to prove that it was unreasonable for the NHS trust to have expected the work to be carried out safely without closing the ward, and that by putting out the notice they took all reasonable care. The person claiming compensation might argue that the notice was not sufficient to ensure that he was safe.

If the injured person was a child, then his representative would argue that section 2(2)(3)(a) of the 1957 Act places a higher duty upon the occupier in relation to a child.

If the injured person was a trespasser, then the relevant provision is the Occupier's Liability Act 1984. Had this been applied to the circumstances described here, it is unlikely that either the NHS trust or the firm of painters would be considered to be liable.

Liability for defective products

Read *Speller*, section 20.6.5, pp. 569-574, which considers the provisions of the Consumer Protection Act 1987. Note when an NHS employee can become a supplier for the purposes of the Act and the significance of this.

7: The four areas of accountability

It should now be possible for you to bring together all the different kinds of laws and regulatory controls which relate to the field of health and safety. These are set out in *Figure 6*.

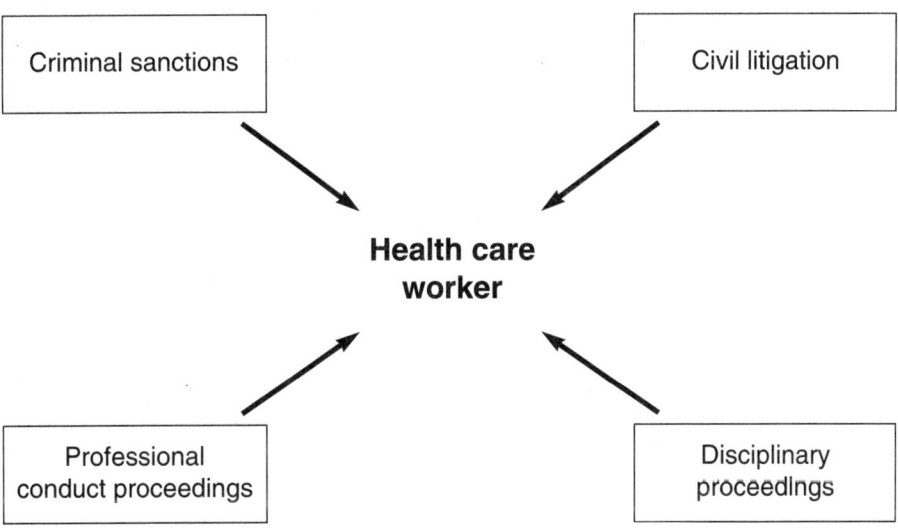

Figure 6: The framework of accountability in health and safety

ACTIVITY 19

ALLOW **10** MINUTES

Answer the following questions in relation to the four areas of accountability: criminal, civil, professional and contractual.

Where do I stand if . . .

1 The system for sterilising is defective:
   ● a patient is infected as a result of the defective sterilising system – who is liable?

2 I am asked to undertake ear syringing for which I have had no training:
   ● a patient suffers severe irreparable damage to the ear – who is liable?

3 The premises are unsafe and unclean:
   ● an elderly patient trips on broken linoleum and fractures her hip – who is liable?

4 I know a colleague to be incompetent:
   ● a colleague has a drink problem and gives the wrong dose of medication to a patient – who is liable?

5 The group fundholding practice introduce minor surgery and I am asked to work as a scrub nurse although I am not trained for this:
   ● a patient is injured as a result of my incompetence – who is liable?

6 I am a community midwife and have to work on an estate known for its violence:
   ● I am injured by a gang of youths who steal my bag – who is liable?

If you are in a non-clinical post, consider some 'What if' questions for yourself and try to answer them.

Commentary

For each area of accountability it should be possible for you to determine whether the different elements required by the different forums of accountability are present. You might find some inconsistencies. It does not follow that because a civil wrong has been established it will also be shown that there is a criminal wrong or that the employee is in breach of contract.

In question **1** there will be liability in the civil, and possibly the criminal, courts of the person responsible for maintaining the safety of the sterilising system. That person could also face disciplinary and professional misconduct proceedings.

In question **2** there could be criminal proceedings, and the patient may also claim compensation from the employer for the negligence of the practitioner who will face professional conduct proceedings for working outside her sphere of competence.

In question **3** the occupier of the premises will be held responsbile for the harm to the patient.

Practitioners cannot ignore potential dangers to patients from colleagues. They should ensure appropriate action is taken by management, disloyal though it may seem to be. However, it is unlikely that the practitioner who failed to report the colleague would be successfully sued in the civil courts, though she may face professional conduct proceedings.

For question **5**, as in question **2**, the practitioner must work within her field of competence and her employer should provide the necessary training for her to become competent in a new field of activity.

Question **6** illustrates that the employer has a duty of care to employees working in the community, and if violence can be foreseen then reasonable steps must be taken to protect the employee. This could include alarms, two-way radios or additional staffing. If the midwife can establish a failure to provide such reasonable protection she may succeed in an action for compensation.

Health and safety laws are constantly being amended to meet higher standards of care and more detailed regulations. This session should have provided you with an understanding of the different sources of law and how each are enforced. Use this understanding to continue to develop your knowledge by keeping up to date with new legislation and regulations and case law.

Summary

● Health and safety law lays down duties on both the employer and the employee.

- The regulations governing health and safety are intended to create a 'health and safety culture'.

- The key stages in health and safety assessment are:

  – assessment

  – review

  – recording

  – prevention and protection.

- Statutory duties including regulations are enforceable through criminal law.

- Civil law, professional codes of conduct and employment contracts also work to regulate health and safety.

Before you move on to Session Four, check that you have achieved the objectives given at the beginning of this session and, if not, review the appropriate sections.

SESSION FOUR

Consent to treatment and research

Introduction

The issue of whether the health professional is entitled to carry out treatment upon the patient is central to the topic of the rights of the patient. Any touching of another person without his consent or other authorisation is a trespass to his person. Touching which is of a social nature is excluded (such as brushing against someone whilst on a crowded train or when queuing to enter a building). Even if the motive behind the touching is altruistic and for that person's benefit (for example, where a surgeon repairs an ingrowing toe nail during an abdominal operation), that is still a trespass if the patient is a mentally competent adult who has not given consent.

The defences to trespass to the person are:

- consent
- necessity
- authorisation by parents
- statutory authorisation.

In this session we will be looking at these defences and the issue of consent to treatment and research.

Session objectives

When you have completed this session, you should be able to:

- describe the legal protection given to the patient against unauthorised interference with his person

- discuss the giving of consent and the procedures to ensure consent is obtained

- explain when there can be interference without the patient's consent

- summarise the legal principles which apply to specific categories such as children and mentally disordered people

- give an account of the Law Commission's proposals regarding anticipatory directives

- discuss the issue of withholding treatment when it can be seen to be in the best interest of the patient to allow him to die

- show an understanding of the role of local research ethics committees.

1: The duty to inform

One of the most important defences to an action for trespass to the person is consent. *Speller*, Chapter 7 covers this topic and the duty to inform the patient which is part of the duty of care in the tort of negligence. There is judicial authority for the view that, if the patient has given consent to treatment, then, in the absence of fraud or duress, an action for trespass will not stand, even when the patient is able to show that he has been given inadequate information concerning the risks of the procedure. If the patient is able to establish that, had that information been made available, he would not have given consent, then the action would be in negligence for breach of the duty to inform. The principles of accountability discussed in Session One then apply.

Read *Speller*, sections 7.2.1, 7.2.2 and 7.2.3, pp. 203-223.

The leading case is the House of Lords' decision in *Sidaway v. Bethlem Royal Hospital Governors* (1985). *Speller* shows that there were divisions in the thinking of the judges but that the majority agreed on the following points:

- English law does not accept the doctrine of informed consent

- the test which should be applied to the giving of information is the Bolam Test (see section 3 of Session One), i.e. 'a doctor is not guilty of negligence if he has acted in accordance with a practice accepted as proper by a responsible body of medical men skilled in that particular art' (Bolam case)

- if the patient asks questions, there is a duty to answer these questions honestly and truthfully.

ACTIVITY 20   ALLOW **20** MINUTES

Study the following cases from *Speller*, section 7.2.3 and then make notes on the questions listed below:

- *Sidaway v. Bethlem Royal Hospital Governors* (1985)

- *Rogers v. Whittaker* (1991) (New South Wales)

- *Chatterton v. Gerson* (1981)

- *Smith v. Auckland Hospital Board* (1965).

1   What were the facts of each case?

2   What was the dispute at issue?

3   What decision was made?

4   What were the reasons for the decision?

If you have time, you might like to look up the actual law report for each case which gives fuller details than are available in *Speller*. Two of the cases are not English and therefore you would have to find a library which kept Australian and New Zealand law reports. The reference for the cases, which is given in *Speller* (note the index of cases on p. xxxii following the Contents), gives you the series of law reports in which it is published, the year of the report, the volume number and the page reference; for example, *Sidaway v. Bethlem Royal Hospital and the Maudsley Governors* 1985 [year] AC [Appeal Courts – no volume number] 871 [page number]. The same case is reported in the All England Reports and the reference is: 1985 [year] 1 [volume] All ER [series] 643 [page].

Commentary

This type of analysis can be used for all the cases which are referred to in this unit. A decision of the House of Lords is binding upon the lower courts unless the facts can be distinguished in some material, i.e. significant, way. In this series of cases, therefore, the House of Lords' decision in *Sidaway* would be the authority for English decisions. The decisions from the Commonwealth courts are of 'persuasive' authority, i.e. they might be cited in the arguments put before the court, but they would not have to be followed.

2: Methods of gaining consent

Consent can be given by non-verbal communication, by word of mouth or in writing.

Non-verbal communication

Non-verbal communication or implied consent is where the patient indicates that he is prepared to agree to an action which would otherwise be a trespass to his person. Thus, rolling up his sleeve for an injection or blood pressure reading, or rolling over to have a pressure sore area rub would all count as non-verbal or implied consent. More debatable is what is implied when the patient comes into hospital. Some have suggested that this implies that the patient is agreeing to surgery or any other treatment for which hospitalisation is necessary. This would, however, be a dangerous assumption, and general consents are similarly of doubtful validity (see *Speller*, p. 208, the last paragraph of section 7.2.2).

Consent by word of mouth

Many health care procedures are given as the result of oral consent. In fact, it is rare for them to require written consent.

Consent in writing

Read *Speller*, **section 7.2.4, pp. 223-231.**

Speller explains clearly that a consent form is *prima facie* evidence that consent has been given. It is not the actual consent. Thus, if a patient who does not have the mental competence to give consent signs a form, the signing does not give to the consent any validity.

Consent by non-verbal communication and by word of mouth are both less reliable as evidence if there is a dispute over whether consent has been given than consent which is evidenced in writing. If any procedure which has risks is being considered, it is therefore preferable to obtain consent in writing. Although this is not necessarily proof that the consent is valid, since there may be evidence to contradict the capacity of the patient to give consent, there is nevertheless a rebuttable presumption that the form is valid and would therefore be a defence against an action for trespass to the person.

ACTIVITY 21   ALLOW 30 MINUTES

Obtain copies of consent forms which are used in your own hospital and compare them with the forms given in *Speller*, pp. 226-230. Are there any significant differences?

Now design a form for consent to community care which would cover the work of a practice nurse, district nurse, community psychiatric nurse or any other community professional. In what circumstances do you think such a form would be of value?

An adult mentally competent patient has the right to take his own discharge, even though contrary to medical advice. Design a form to be signed by such a patient before he leaves hospital care. The form should also make provision in the event that the patient refuses to sign it.

Commentary

Most hospitals have forms for consent to treatment which follow the NHS Management Executive (1990) guidelines. Some, however, have developed forms for particular procedures and specific categories of patients. For example, section 3(5) of the Children Act 1989 permits a person who does not have parental responsibility for the child but has care of the child to do what is reasonable in all the circumstances of the case for the purpose of safeguarding or promoting the child's welfare. Thus, accident and emergency departments could have provision on a form, in relation to the emergency treatment of a child, for a non-parent in the circumstances envisaged by section 3(5) to give consent to treatment.

A form which covers the situation where a patient takes his own discharge contrary to medical advice needs to state this explicitly. In the event of the patient refusing to sign the form, two witnesses should sign that they heard the patient being advised to stay in hospital but that he refused to accept this advice and insisted on taking his own discharge. The signatories should give their full name, their position in the hospital and the date and time of their signing the form.

3: The unconscious patient

In certain situations it is impracticable to obtain the consent of the patient. A clear example of this is where the person is unconscious but requires life-saving treatment.

Read *Speller*, **section 7.2.8, pp. 235-236.**

Emergency treatment

The relatives do not have any right in law to withhold consent where the adult is unconscious. In such cases the professional acts according to his professional duty, following the Bolam Test, and, out of necessity, provides emergency life-saving treatment. Necessity in such circumstances would justify emergency life-saving treatment but not elective treatment for which there was no overriding need. Judicial authority for such action is discussed in the case of *Re F v. Berkshire Health Authority,* which is considered in section 5 of this session.

Blood transfusions

The principles in law applying to the giving of blood are no different from those applying in the provision of any other treatment. If the mentally competent adult refuses blood, then it is a trespass to his person to give him blood, but if he is unable to consent, the same conditions would apply as in the previous paragraph.

Advance directives

If the person is unconscious but is carrying a card that purports to refuse blood or blood products, then, in the absence of any evidence which would cast doubt on its validity, that refusal should be accepted. The Canadian case of *Malette v. Schulman* (1990) has no direct English counterpart, but there is judicial support in English cases (see the Tony Bland case and Re T (1992)).

In the Canadian case, the court held that because the patient was carrying a card which made it clear that he refused to accept blood products, then the doctor should have accepted that and not given blood even in a life-saving situation. The patient was, therefore, awarded compensation against the doctor. Thus the card was regarded as a 'living will' or 'advance directive' by the patient to govern a time at which he would be unable to make his views known directly. However, in England, in the absence of an Act of Parliament which covers the situation relating to living wills or advance directives, many questions arise which have no clear answers:

1 What should be the legal effect of a card as in the Canadian case?

2 What formalities should be required to make any advance directive binding?

3 Could an advance directive cover every aspect of treatment; e.g. could a person refuse food?

4 Once an advance directive has been set up, how could it be ended? By simply tearing it up?

5 How should it be communicated to others? Should there be a system of registration?

6 How should the professions be protected if they obey an advance directive?

63

7   Should there be any penalties if they ignore one?

8   What should the penalties be if an advance directive is falsified or forged?

ACTIVITY 22   ALLOW 20 MINUTES

Imagine that you wish to draw up a living will to express your views about what should happen if there should be a time when you are not able to communicate to the professionals. Draft a document which you consider would be valid for such an eventuality. As you do this, try to answer the above questions so that your document would have legal force and validity, and the scope of the law would cover what you intend to include in your living will.

Commentary

Most of the above questions were discussed in the Law Commission's consultation paper, *Mentally Incapacitated Adults and Decision-Making: Medical Treatment and Research* (The Law Commission, 1993b). Their recommendations in relation to the questions asked in this activity are given below.

1   What should be the legal effect of an anticipatory directive?

The Law Commission (1993b, para. 3.13) recommended that, if a patient is incapacitated (as defined in their report), a clearly established anticipatory decision should be as effective as the contemporaneous decision of the patient would be in the circumstances to which it is applicable. In other words, just as a refusal by the patient to treatment offered by a professional is effective in preventing the giving of treatment, so a refusal provided earlier should be effective.

2   What formalities should be required?

This is difficult, since the easier it is for the patient to make his views known about future treatment, the more danger there is that fraud could take place. The Law Commission (1993b, para. 3.19) recommended that there should be a rebuttable presumption that an anticipatory decision is clearly established if it is in writing, signed by the maker, with appropriate provision for signing at his direction, and witnessed by one person who is not the maker's medical treatment attorney. This means that the refusal to have treatment conveyed by others would not be effective.

3   Could an advance directive cover all treatments, including food?

The Law Commission (1993b, para. 3.26) recommended that an anticipatory decision should be regarded as ineffective to the extent that it purports to refuse pain relief or 'basic care', including nursing care and spoon-feeding. This, like all its other recommendations, is subject to consultation. It is likely to be a contentious area, since some people may want their wishes for the future to include the refusal of food so that they are allowed to die more quickly. However, this refusal would be extremely difficult for professionals to accept.

4   How could it be ended?

The Law Commission recommended (1993b, para. 3.34) that an anticipatory decision could be revoked (i.e. withdrawn) orally or in writing at any time when the maker has the capacity to do so (according to the test proposed in Part II of Consultation Paper No. 128, The Law Commission, 1993a). There should be no automatic revocation after a period of time and no additional formalities should be required. It would therefore be easier to bring an advance directive to an end than to initiate one.

5   How should it be communicated to others?

It is essential that professional staff have early notification of the views of a patient expressed through an advance directive. Since it must be in writing the patient should carry it around with him. If he is hospitalised when he is competent he should bring it to the notice of the ward staff. It is also essential that members of his immediate family should be aware of his wishes. Registration, such as has been proposed regarding organ donation, may not be effective in providing a sufficiently speedy response and failure to register should not be an obstacle to ensuring that the patient's wishes are respected.

6   How should the professionals be protected if they obey an advance directive?

The Law Commission recommended (1993b, para. 3.35) that a treatment provider who acts in accordance with an apparently valid and continuing anticipatory decision should only be liable to any civil or criminal proceedings if he does so in bad faith or without reasonable care. This protection would cover the situation where it is subsequently discovered that the anticipatory decision had been withdrawn.

7   Should there be any penalties for ignoring an advance directive?

Clearly, the whole basis of the thinking behind the recognition of advance directives is that the patient's wishes should prevail and it cannot be within the discretion of an individual professional whether or not he will abide by the patient's views. Where the professional ignores a valid advance directive he would be liable to the same legal actions as where he ignores a valid refusal (i.e. trespass to the person, assault and battery).

8   What should the penalties be if an advance directive is falsified or forged?

The Law Commission (1993b, para. 3.36) recommends that it should be an offence to falsify or forge an advance directive, or to conceal, alter or destroy a directive without the authority of its maker. These offences should apply to a written revocation of an advance directive as they do to the directive itself.

The Law Commission (1991, 1993a, 1993b, 1993c, 1995) recommended that there should be an Act of Parliament to provide the framework and legal basis for anticipatory decisions. The recommendations should be seen in the wider context of the issues relating to decision-making by the mentally incompetent adult. Their proposals have significant implications for all practitioners. The Select Committee on Medical Ethics of the House of Lords supports these recommendations. It does not consider legislation is necessary, but suggests that a code of practice should be developed (House of Lords, 1994).

4: The minor

Read *Speller*, **section 7.3, up to the end of 7.3.1, pp. 241-244.**

The minor of 16 and 17

Section 8 of the Family Law Reform Act 1968 covers the situation of consent to treatment by the 16 and 17 year old. Note sections 8(1) and 8(2) and the definition of medical treatment for the purposes of the Act. A professional who relies upon the consent of the 16 or 17 year old to treatment, diagnostic procedure or anaesthetic would have a defence to an action for trespass.

However, section 8(3) upholds the validity of any consent which would have been effective had this Act not been passed. This can have two meanings: on the one hand, it can enable a mature minor under 16 to give a valid consent; on the other hand, it would validate the giving of consent on behalf of the minor of 16 or 17 by his parents.

In the case of *Re W (a minor)(medical treatment)* (1992) (discussed in *Speller* p. 243), the Court of Appeal held that the minor of 16 could be given treatment against her will. It drew a distinction between the giving of consent (authorised for the 16 and 17 year old by the Family Law Reform Act) and the withholding of consent. In the latter case, the refusal of the child could be overruled when it was in her best interests so to do. It referred to the Childrens Act 1989 and the principle that the child's wishes should be taken into account in treatment decisions, and said that its decision was not contrary to the legislation.

Minors under 16 years

Read *Speller*, sections 7.3.2 and 7.3.3, pp. 244–259.

The decision of the House of Lords in the Gillick case is the leading authority on the right of the minor under 16 years to give consent to treatment. The courts recognise that weight must be attached to the maturity of the minor and his understanding of the situation. There is no specific age at which the minor can be said to lack or have competence. This is in accord with the philosophy of the Children Act 1989, which states as a basic principle that in determining whether specific orders should be made under section 1(4) of the Act, 'a court shall have regard in particular to: (a) the ascertainable wishes and feelings of the child concerned (considered in the light of his age and understanding) (Section 1(3))'.

ACTIVITY 23
ALLOW **30** MINUTES

With reference to *Speller*, sections 7.3.2 and 7.3.3, which you have just read, answer the following questions, quoting where possible the name of the case which gives authority for your answer.

1 A child who is under 16 needs a blood transfusion as a matter of life and death. The parents are Jehovah's Witnesses and refuse to give consent. Can a doctor give blood to the child without the order of a court?

2 The facts are similar to those in question 1, but before the doctor can administer the blood the child dies. What action, if any, can then be taken against the parents?

3 A mature child of 15 years is pregnant and wants to have an abortion. She does not want her parents to be told. Assuming that the statutory requirements of the Abortion Act 1967 are met, can she give consent in her own right? If the parents hear about the abortion, could they prevent it going ahead by offering to take care of the baby?

4 A baby is born with Down's syndrome and has other serious congenital disabilities. It is clear that an abdominal operation is necessary to save

his life. The parents do not wish to give consent to this operation. The doctors wish to proceed with the operation since it is their view that if the operation were to proceed the child would have a reasonable quality of life, even though he will suffer from severe learning disabilities. What is the parents' position in law? What action should the doctors take?

5 The father of a girl of 14 has been charged with sexual abuse. The girl refuses to agree to a medical assessment. Without this the prosecution consider that they are unable to secure a conviction. What is the legal position?

Commentary

1 The court has the power to act in the best interests of the child and, if appropriate, to order the blood transfusion to proceed. Note that if there is too little time to obtain a court order, the doctors can proceed and follow the Bolam Test by acting in the best interests of the child, according to the decision in *Re F* which we will be looking at in the next section.

2 There have been successful prosecutions of parents in this situation and the text quotes the case of *R. v Senior* 1989 (*Speller*, p. 248).

3 If the child has the capacity she can consent to the abortion. The parents do not have the right to prevent it taking place if the legal requirements set down by the Abortion Act 1967 (as amended) are satisfied, whether or not they offer to take care of the baby. In the case of *Re P* (*a minor*) 1982, the judge (Mrs Justice Butler-Sloss) ordered that the termination of pregnancy should proceed. After discussions with the girl, she formed the view that the girl was of a strong personality and mature views and that the statutory requirements were satisfied (*Speller*, pp. 249-250).

4 In the case of in *Re B* (*a minor*) 1981, the Court of Appeal ordered the operation to proceed. The doctors had a duty to act in the best interests of the child (*Speller*, p. 251).

5 Under the Children Act 1989, the child may refuse to submit to an examination or other assessment if she is of sufficient understanding to make an informed decision, even though the court has ordered it (Section 44(7) and Section 43(8)) (*Speller* pp. 244 and 259).

5: Mentally disordered persons

Read *Speller*, section 7.5, pp. 263-268.

There are two ways in which treatment of a mentally disordered adult can proceed if he is incapable of giving consent:

1 Part 4 of the Mental Health Act 1983 covers the giving of treatment for mental disorder to certain detained patients under the Mental Health Act 1983, and sets out the provisions for giving them treatment in the absence of consent. It does not cover treatments for physical disorder. (Session Eight discusses the provisions of the Act in more detail).

2 The doctrine of necessity enables a person to take action in the best interests of a person who is unable to give consent.

The leading case is the House of Lords' decision in *Re F* (1989) (*Speller*, pp. 263-4); advice is also given in the NHS Management Executive's (1990) *A Guide to Consent for Examination and Treatment*. Whilst *Re F* was concerned with consent for sterilisation, the decision has been held to apply to care and treatment given by professionals to adults who lack the mental capacity to give consent. Provided that professionals act according to the Bolam Test in the best interests of the patient, they should not be acting unlawfully.

However, *Re F* has raised many uncertainties, such as:

- would it extend to the situation where the patient was actively refusing treatment and care, rather than just passively accepting it without consent?

- which professionals can rely upon it?

- what rights do carers have if there is a dispute between them and the professionals as to what is in the best interests of the client?

The Law Commission (1993b, 1995) has recommended that there should be legislation to establish a framework for decision-making on behalf of incapacitated adults. The framework would include a statutory power to treat in such circumstances. It also recommended that there should be provision for the judicial authorisation of both specific orders and general orders in relation to treatment.

As was pointed out above, the Mental Health Act 1983 does not cover the giving of treatment for physical disorder. If, therefore, a chronic schizophrenic patient refused to have a life-saving operation for appendicitis, there is no statutory power to perform the operation. It could be done on the basis of *Re F* or, if there were time, there could be an application to the courts. Because of the difficulties, the Mental Health Act Commission drafted an occasional paper, *Consent to Treatment* (MHAC, 1985), which is set out in *Speller*, pp. 268-273, section 7.6. This guidance does not have any legal effect and, once the recommendations of the Law Commission (1993b) are made law, will be superseded. However, for the present, the paper provides useful guidelines.

In the case of *Re C* (*Adult*) (*Refusal of Medical Treatment*) (Family Division (1994) 1 All ER 819), a patient at Broadmoor Special Hospital who suffered from chronic schizophrenia obtained an injunction to prevent the hospital carrying out an operation to amputate his foot without his consent. He was suffering from gangrene and his doctors advised that amputation was in his best interests as a life-saving necessity. It was held, however, that he had the capacity to understand the situation and his refusal to consent was valid.

6: Withdrawal of treatment from incompetent adults

Speller, pp. 274-275, section 7.6.1, covers the situation which existed in the case of Tony Bland and the House of Lords' decision which permitted the artificial feeding to be stopped. It was held to be in the best interests of the patient to be allowed to die.

Under English law euthanasia is unlawful. This means that it is unlawful to cause the death of a person even with the consent of that person. You may be aware of the case in which Dr Nigel Cox was successfully prosecuted for causing the death of a patient by giving her potassium chloride, and sentenced to one year's imprisonment suspended for one year.

ACTIVITY 24   ALLOW 15 MINUTES

What do you consider are the legal differences between the Cox case and the Bland case?

Earlier in this session we discussed the issues around advance directives and living wills. Bearing that in mind, do you consider that a professional who, in accordance with your previously declared wishes, failed to resuscitate you following a heart attack has carried out an act of euthanasia?

Make a list of what criteria you think should be used in deciding what is in the best interests of the patient.

Commentary

In the case of Tony Bland, treatment was withheld on the basis that the courts do not have to prolong the life of a patient if it could be said to be in the best interests of the patient to be allowed to die. However, there is a distinction in law between letting the patient die and causing the death of the patient. The inquest on Tony Bland held that death was caused by the injuries sustained in the football tragedy, i.e. the cessation of feeding was not seen as a cause of death. In the Nigel Cox case, the administration of potassium chloride was given with intent to cause the death of the patient. The distinction is one which some philosophers of ethics in health care have questioned (Glover, 1977; Harris, 1985).

In accepting the refusal of a mentally competent patient to receive life-saving treatment, a doctor is not committing an act of murder. Similarly, in the event of a professional accepting a lawfully made advance directive refusing treatment prepared by a patient who is no longer competent, that acceptance would not be regarded as an act of murder.

The criteria for what is in the best interests of the patient must be drawn up on the basis of an objective assessment of the actions which would produce the most favourable outcome for the patient. Thus 'best interests' have to be distinguished from what is known as a 'substituted judgement' test, where a decision is made on the basis of what the patient would have chosen had he had the capacity to do so. The distinction is important in such decisions as the giving of an organ for transplant. It could be said to be not in his best interests for a mentally incompetent person to donate an organ such as a kidney to a sibling. If the substituted judgement test were to be applied, however, it might well be that the person would wish to make such an altruistic gift.

7: Consent in teaching and research

Read *Speller*, section 7.7, pp. 275-283.

Patients are used in clinical teaching, but such use should be with their consent. The Patients' Charter suggests that they should be notified by the hospital that it is a teaching hospital and their consent obtained. Guidance is also given in the circular, *Teaching on Patients* (DHSS, 1973). Patients should also be able to give or withhold consent to research. Research in medical and other areas is now subject to the guidelines issued by the Department of Health in relation to the function and appointment of local research ethics committees. These have a duty to ensure that the consent of the patient is obtained. The Medical Research Council has set out guidelines for investigations on human subjects and these can be found in *Speller*, pp. 283-288. The legal restrictions on research after death are examined in Session Nine.

ALLOW **20** MINUTES

Obtain a copy of the procedure and practice of your local research ethics committee (LREC) and answer the following questions:

1 Who are the members of the LREC?

2 Who appoints them?

3 What is their function?

4 If there is a situation where the LREC has given approval to a research project and a patient subsequently complains that her consent was not obtained, will the consent of the LREC protect the doctor against an action for trespass to the person?

5 Do you consider that the role of the LREC could be widened to include decision-making in situations such as Tony Bland's or in cases such as those you read earlier (*Speller*, pp. 251-255): *Re C (a minor) (wardship: medical treatment)* (1989); *Re J (a minor) (wardship: medical treatment)* (1990) and *Re J (a minor) (wardship: medical treatment)* (1992)? Give reasons for your answer.

Commentary

The details obtained from your LREC should give you the answers to the first three questions.

The approval of the LREC for research to proceed does not act as a substitute for the consent of the patient herself if she is mentally competent. One of the functions of the LREC is to ensure that the researchers have obtained the informed consent of the persons who are to take part in the research.

Whether the role of the LREC could be extended to make decisions of a wider nature than the present functions is highly debatable. The proposals of the Law Commission (1993b, 1995) on decision-making on behalf of the mentally incompetent adult do not envisage that the LRECs would have a role in this type of decision-making. Such a decision being made by a committee would give rise to problems of accountability; could it, for example, be made by a majority?

Summary

● A mentally competent adult cannot be compelled to have treatment against his will. Such an act would be known as a trespass to his person.

● Sufficient information must be given to the patient before consent is obtained for the duty of care to be fulfilled.

● Where it is impracticable to obtain the consent of the patient, the professionals can give treatment under the Bolam Test, unless the patient has left written instructions to the contrary.

- Specific provisions apply to children and adults who lack mental capacity.

- Local research ethics committees ensure that ethical guidelines are followed in the carrying out of research.

Before you move on to Session Five, check that you have achieved the objectives given at the beginning of this session and, if not, review the appropriate sections.

SESSION FIVE

Standards for confidentiality and record-keeping

Introduction

The aim of this session is to explore the duty of confidentiality, including the issue of so-called 'whistle-blowing' and how it can be handled. We will look at the provisions of the Data Protection Act 1984 and at the right of access to records and reports held in manual form. The session ends with a discussion of who owns records and the need for them to be clear and comprehensive.

Session objectives

When you have completed this session, you should be able to:

● describe the duty of confidentiality in relation to information obtained from patients

● explain the statutory provisions governing the keeping, disclosure and access to personal data under the Data Protection Act 1984

● discuss the access to health records held in manual form under the Access to Health Records Act 1990 and access to medical reports prepared for employment or insurance purposes given by the Access to Medical Reports Act 1988

● summarise the legal requirements relating to the ownership and preservation of records.

1: The duty of confidentiality

Read *Speller*, **Chapter 16, sections 16.1 and 16.2, pp. 390-392.**

The nature of the obligation

Note that the obligation of confidentiality on health care professionals has two sources:

- moral: as expressed in the Hippocratic Oath, which can be acted upon by professional bodies

- legal: see the case of *Furniss v. Fitchett* (1958), for example, which suggests that, if harm arises as a result of a breach of confidence, the plaintiff could claim through the tort of negligence.

There is usually an express clause in the contract of employment for health care workers requiring the employee to recognise the duty of confidentiality. In the absence of an express term, the courts would probably imply a term to the effect that confidentiality must be respected in order to make business sense of the contract. Similarly, in the case of private patient care, the courts may recognise the existence of an implied term in the contract between private practitioner and patient, even if there is not an express term prohibiting disclosure.

'Whistle-blowing'

The issue of confidentiality has come to the fore in recent years in relation to 'whistle-blowing'. The case of Graham Pink is an illustration (Turner, 1990). He was dismissed from his post as night nurse after he had approached *The Guardian* newspaper with details of information relating to patient care. One of the reasons given for his dismissal was that he was in breach of confidentiality by giving information to the media. The case was eventually settled when the authority learnt that costs were likely to exceed £250,000. There is as yet no judicial authority on the question as to when disclosure to the media is a justifiable action on the part of an employee.

In 1993 the NHS Management Executive issued guidelines for staff on relations with the public and the media; this is reproduced as Resource 5.

ACTIVITY 26　　　　　　　　　ALLOW 30 MINUTES

Read *Resource 5* and then tackle the following questions:

1　Paragraph 6 states that under no circumstances are employees who express their views about health service issues in accordance with this guidance to be penalised in any way for doing so. If you were a senior manager, what measures would you introduce to protect staff according to this principle?

2　Paragraphs 8 and 9 stress the responsibilities of staff in maintaining confidentiality. What measures would you take to ensure that each employee recognises this duty of confidentiality?

3　The guidance recommends the setting up of local procedures for dealing with staff concerns. What specific features do you consider your own local procedure should show? Why are local procedures necessary, rather than just a nationally set procedure?

4   Obtain a copy of your own local procedure and compare it with the circular.

Commentary

With the development of the internal market within the NHS and increasing pressures on public expenditure, managers should ensure that staff are able to make their concerns about hazards to patient care known to senior management; they should therefore ensure that opportunity is given to staff to discuss any concerns without fear of victimisation. The procedures recommended in the circular should be followed. A clear grievance procedure should be implemented to protect any member of staff who raises concerns in accordance with the guidance. At the same time, the right of the patient to confidentiality should be protected. Education as to the right of the patient for information concerning him and received from him to be kept confidential should therefore be provided for staff, and should be regularly reinforced through practice and procedures.

Local procedures can deal with specific fields of accountability that are of concern locally, and identify officers to be responsible for implementing and monitoring procedures.

Exceptions to the duty of confidentiality

Read *Speller*, sections 16.3 to 16.9, pp. 392-411 and section 5.3, pp. 134-146. Make notes on the circumstances when exceptions to the duty of confidentiality apply.

There are a number of circumstances when the duty of confidentiality does not apply.

The patient's consent
As the obligation of confidentiality is owed to the patient, he is therefore free to give consent to any disclosure (*Speller*, 16.2).

Infectious diseases
There is a statutory obligation relating to the notification of infectious disease. There is also provision in the NHS (Venereal Diseases) Regulations 1974 for both notification and confidentiality. Note that there is judicial authority to suggest that AIDS is included in the scope of these Regulations (*Speller*, 16.3).

Compulsion of law

1   There is no privilege in court against disclosure of confidential information obtained from a patient. If the information is relevant to a matter before the court, then the health professional who received it from the patient can be subpoenaed to give evidence and he cannot claim professional privilege against disclosure. See the case of *A-G v. Mulholland and Foster* (1963) (*Speller* 16.4.1).

2   There is a duty to give information to the police under the Road Traffic Regulation Act 1984, section 112. See the details of the case of *Hunter v. Mann* (1974) (*Speller* 16.4.2).

3 The Prevention of Terrorism Act 1989, section 18, requires the notification to the police of information which would be of material assistance in relation to the investigation of terrorist activities (this is not covered in *Speller*).

4 Under the Supreme Court Act 1981, sections 33 and 34, information can be ordered to be disclosed to a party who is either already involved in litigation or likely to be so (*Speller* 5.3).

Disclosure in the interest of the public

All professional codes of practice recognise that, in certain exceptional circumstances, disclosure of confidential information may be justified in the greater interests of the public. If you have access to the advisory papers of the UKCC, look at its advisory paper on confidentiality (UKCC, 1987) which provides useful guidance on the procedures which should be followed if a practitioner is faced with the dilemma of whether or not to breach patient confidentiality. Extracts from the advice given by the Medical Defence Union and the British Medical Association are quoted in *Speller*, pp. 402-403, section 16.5.1.

Minors

The law relating to the giving of confidential information obtained from minors to their parents is parallel to that relating to consent to treatment in the same circumstances. If the minor is sufficiently mature and understands the situation, then, if the elements laid down in *Gillick* are satisfied, the minor's information can be treated in confidence and not relayed to the parents.

Information concerning a will

The professional has a duty to keep the making of a will by a patient confidential and, if he is aware of them, the dispositions under the will. Clearly, in the event of the death of the patient, the existence of a will should be made known to the personal representatives.

AIDS

In the case of *X (Health Authority) v. Y and others* (1988) the conclusion reached was that the plaintiffs were entitled to a permanent injunction restraining the defendants from publishing confidential information identifying the two doctors as AIDS sufferers (*Speller* 16.8).

Information by an examining psychiatrist

In the case of *W. v. Egdell and others* (1990), the court considered that the circumstances justified disclosure on grounds of public interest (*Speller* 16.9).

ACTIVITY 27　　　　　　ALLOW 15 MINUTES

Read through the following list of circumstances and assess whether there is lawful justification for disclosure in each case. Where you think there is, give the source of the legal authority for disclosure.

1 A minor of 15 tells the paediatric nurse that she is being sexually abused by her father but does not want her mother told.

2 The wife of a patient phones to find out how her husband is progressing after a serious operation.

3 An accident and emergency nurse is asked by the police to tell him the name and address of the passengers in a car crash. Both passengers have been injured and admitted to hospital.

4   A patient is suing the driver of a car in which he was injured. The driver claims that the patient already had a serious heart condition and therefore his claim should be reduced on those grounds. The driver asks the hospital to produce the records of the patient for him to see.

5   A husband phones the VD clinic to find out when his wife's next appointment is, as she has forgotten it.

6   A volunteer who is taking a person with severe learning disabilities on a day's excursion asks if he could see the client's medical records before he goes.

7   A surgeon discovers that he is HIV positive and tells his friend, also a surgeon. He refuses to let anyone else know.

8   A film star, who has just won an Oscar, is admitted to hospital. The press phone up to check on his progress.

Commentary

1   The paediatric nurse would in these circumstances have to ensure that the area child protection committee was informed of the danger to the child and this would necessarily entail that the mother was informed. In certain circumstances the local authority might have to consider the possibility of using some of the provisions of the Children Act 1989 to protect the child.

2   The nurse should check with the husband as to whether he wishes his wife to be notified of his progress because the duty of confidentiality is owed to the patient. There may be reasons why the husband does not wish this information given, of which the nurse might not be aware. If the patient is incapable of making a decision, then a close relative can be notified in the patient's best interests.

3   There is a statutory duty for this information to be given to the police. The nurse should of course confirm that it is in fact the police if the conversation is by phone. The normal procedure would be for the police to come to the department and the consultant or manager in charge would give the statutorily authorised information.

4   An application could be made under section 34(2) of the Supreme Court Act 1981 for disclosure to be made against someone who is not a party to the proceedings. This could be done after the writ had been issued.

5   Disclosure would not be justified in these circumstances unless the clerk had written evidence that the wife agreed to the information being passed on.

6   Disclosure would be justified, in the interests of the client and the health and safety of the volunteer, of such information as was necessary to ensure that both client and volunteer were safe. This might be, for instance, information that the client suffered from epilepsy and instructions to the volunteer how to deal with a fit.

7   The guidelines issued by the Department of Health (NHS Management Executive, 1994) now apply and the employee should notify his employers. Should he fail to do so, a colleague would probably be justified in passing on the information in the public interest.

8   No information can be disclosed without the consent of the patient in such circumstances.

2: The Data Protection Act 1984

Speller, **Chapter 13, sets out the principles of the Data Protection Act 1984. Skim through the chapter, pp. 350-370, noting as you do so the points listed below.**

1   Application of the Act

The Act only applies to information which can be processed automatically and which makes it possible to identify a living individual (sections 13.1.1; 13.1.2; 13.1.3).

2   Definitions

Note the definition of data users and data subjects (sections 13.2.1; 13.2.2; 13.2.3).

3   Exempt data

There are several categories of data exempt from the provisions of the Act, and those relevant to health care are set out in section 13.3.

4   The Data Protection Registrar

The Data Protection Registrar maintains a register of all those data users who hold personal data. The details of registration and procedure for applications are given in section 13.4.

5   The principles of data protection

Take careful note of the main principles of data protection which are summarised below. Data should be

● obtained and processed fairly and lawfully

● held for lawful purposes only

● disclosed only as appropriate for the purpose held

● adequate, relevant and not excessive

● accurate and up to date

● held not longer than necessary

● known, accessible and capable of amendment or correction

● properly secured.

Further details are given in *Speller*, section 13.5.

6   Non-disclosure exemptions

The exemptions mentioned in point **3** above are those that are completely exempt from the Act. The exemptions discussed in section 13.6 of *Speller* apply only to the restrictions on disclosure; i.e. they allow data users to disclose data in the circumstances given.

7   Sanctions and penalties for breach of the Act

The registrar can issue enforcement notices and de-registration notices if there is a failure to comply with the principles. She can also issue a transfer prohibition (section 13.6.8).

8 Rights of data subjects

Section 21 of the Act gives the data subject the statutory right of access to personal data. In the context of health care, this right of access is modified by a statutory instrument; see Data Protection (Subject Access Modification) (Health) Order 1987 discussed under the heading 'Health and social work' in *Speller*, pp. 365-367. Note the circumstances when access can be withheld. A similar statutory instrument exists in relation to social work information.

9 Compensation

The data subject can claim compensation for:

● inaccuracy

● unauthorised loss or disclosure

and can seek rectification and erasure.

ACTIVITY 28   ALLOW **20** MINUTES

In the Introduction you were asked to obtain the Data Protection Registrar's Annual Report and a pack of information covering the Act, the regulations and the role of the Registrar. Have a look through the material you have received. In the pack you will see the forms for application to be registered as a data user and the procedures which must be followed.

If you were unable to obtain a copy of the pack, contact the officer responsible for the registration of information under the Act in your authority and ask him about his function within the authority.

For what purposes should a health authority or trust be registered in relation to patients, staff and other personal computerised records?

Commentary

From the pack you should have been able to find out the procedure for registering under the Act, the principles that must be followed and the sanctions which can be brought against anyone who fails to follow the principles. If you have made contact with the person responsible for registration within your organisation, you should have found out for what purposes registration has been made and how the officer ensures compliance with the Act within your organisation.

3: Access to health records and medical reports held in manual form

Access to health records

The Access to Health Records Act 1990 removed the anomaly whereby patients had a statutory right of access to their health records if they were in computerised form but not if they were held in manual form. Access to manually held records was brought into force for all records held after 1 November 1991, unless access to records before that date is necessary to make sense of records made later. The provisions for exclusion are similar to those under the Data Protection Access to Health Records Statutory Instrument. The Access to Health Records Act does not apply to records held in computerised form. Thus the two pieces of legislation are mutually exclusive.

Read *Speller*, Chapter 14, pp. 373-380, taking note of the points listed below.

---

1   The definition of health professional for the purposes of the Act (section 14.1). It does not include social worker and access to records made by or on behalf of a social worker is covered by the Access to Personal Files Statutory Instrument.

2   Who may apply for access.

3   How to make the application.

4   The responsibilities of the health service body.

5   Safeguards and exemptions.

6   There are no charges for records made within the last 40 days, except for photocopying and postage.

7   Enforcement.

ACTIVITY 29   ALLOW **20 MINUTES**

Answer the following questions:

1   Access to health records can be denied if serious harm would be caused to the physical or mental well-being of the patient. How would you define serious harm? Give examples of the kind of serious harm which you think would justify withholding records from the patient.

2   Each patient's application for access must be dealt with individually, but are there any categories of record which you consider are more likely to be withheld than others?

3   Do you have any concerns or problems in dealing with this statutory right of access?

4   Are there any ways in which you think the statutory right could be of benefit to your work as a health professional/manager?

5   Is the right of access likely to affect your record-keeping?

6 Can you identify any ways in which the right of access could be a positive benefit to the patient?

Commentary

The answers to these questions in the main relate to your personal understanding of the legislation and how you see it affecting your practice and those of your colleagues. There has as yet been no judicial decision about the meaning of serious harm to the physical or mental health of the patient or another, and therefore it is still a matter for conjecture as to how those terms will be defined. What is clear, however, is that each case will be decided upon its own merits and there will not be a ruling which states that those being cared for by a particular specialty will not be able to have access to their records.

If you have answered 'yes' to question **3**, you should identify your concerns and take them up with the relevant person in your organisation. Thus, if, for example, your concern is with writing records which are too frank and may offend a patient, take this up with your senior manager. If you are concerned about exclusion of access, take this up with the holder of the records, probably the unit manager.

Access to Medical Reports Act 1988

This Act is far more limited in scope than the other legislation we have been covering. It gives the patient a statutory right of access to a report prepared by the patient's own doctor for employment or insurance purposes. If the employer or an insurance company were to ask another independent doctor to carry out the examination, the Act does not apply; however, the patient, who would have to agree to such an examination, could agree on the understanding that he would receive a copy of the report and that the report would not be sent to anyone else without his prior consent.

The Act contains exemptions to access similar to those in the other statutes. If the patient disagrees with any part of the report he can ask for this to be changed and the practitioner can then either amend it or, if he disagrees with the request, he can attach to the report a statement of the individual's views in respect of any part of the report that he is declining to amend. This Act is covered in section 14.2 of *Speller*.

4: Ownership and preservation of records

Read *Speller*, **Chapter 15, pp. 382-389.**

Ownership

There is a difference between the ownership of NHS records and private patient records. The former are the property of the statutory authority for whom the professional was working at the time they were made. The records which a general practitioner is obliged by his terms of service to keep must be returned to the Family Health Services Authority (FHSA) when the patient dies or transfers to another practice. In contrast, where a patient is seen by a practitioner acting in a private capacity, then the records are owned by the practitioner.

Storage

Note the provisions of the Public Records Act 1958 and, in particular, circular HC(89) 20 (*Speller*, section 15.3).

Records as evidence in court proceedings

You may recall from our discussion on confidentiality in section 1 of this session that health records are not privileged from disclosure in court. If records are relevant to an issue arising in a court case, whether civil or criminal, disclosure and production in court can be ordered. This means that any person whose work involves the recording of information must be aware of the possibility of these records being examined in connection with court proceedings. It is essential that they should be comprehensive, clear, unambiguous and capable of withstanding the passing of time, since they may not be called into evidence until several years after they were made. The writer of the records might then be summoned to give evidence which would be used to determine the weight that could be attached to the records.

ACTIVITY 30   ALLOW 30 MINUTES

Read *Standards for Records and Record Keeping* (UKCC, 1993) which you were asked to obtain for this activity and refer to it as you tackle the following:

1 With a group of colleagues, identify any weaknesses in your own system of record-keeping and consider ways it could be improved.

2 What do you consider are the essential principles that should be followed in recording information?

Commentary

Hopefully, this activity will have assisted you in identifying any specific weaknesses which exist in the system you use and how they can be eradicated. The UKCC guidance should be followed. It is appropriate to all records kept on patient care and treatment, whether or not you are a registered practitioner.

Summary

- Managers should ensure that staff are able to express any concerns about patient care to senior management without fear of victimisation.

- There is a duty of confidentiality on health care professionals, but there are a number of circumstances when it can be overridden.

- All data users who hold personal data must be registered with the Data Protection Registrar.

- There has been statutory right of access to computerised data and written medical records since 1 November 1991.

- The courts can ask to see health records so it is important that they are clear, comprehensive and will stand the passage of time.

Before you move on to Session Six, check that you have achieved the objectives given at the beginning of this session and, if not, review the appropriate sections.

The statutory framework for health care and the handling of complaints

Introduction

The aim of this session is to look at the statutory duties placed on the Secretary of State for Health by the National Health Service Act 1977 and to review the machinery through which health care is commissioned and delivered. The significant changes introduced by the National Health Service and Community Care Act 1990 will also be considered.

In this session we will be working through Chapter 2 of *Speller*, 'Hospitals managed under the National Health Service Act 1977' and Chapter 8, 'Complaints in the National Health Service'. Chapter 3 covers voluntary hospitals and Chapter 4 the registration and inspection of nursing homes, and the Registered Homes Tribunal. We will not be looking at these chapters in this unit as we are concentrating on the law relating to the NHS hospitals, but you may like to read them at your convenience if these areas are of interest to you.

Session objectives

When you have completed this session you should be able to:

- explain the statutory basis of authorities within the NHS and the duties of these authorities to provide health care

- discuss the implications of the introduction of the internal market and the purchaser/provider divide

- outline the legal machinery for the enforcement of duties through an action for breach of statutory duty, the complaints mechanisms and the default procedures

- give an account of the handling of clinical and non-clinical complaints by or on behalf of hospital patients

- summarise the role and powers of the Health Service Commissioner and of the Mental Health Act Commission.

1: The statutory duty to provide health care

For the most part there is no absolute duty on the Secretary of State to provide health care; much is left to her discretion. This is essential. Demand for health services will always exceed supply and decisions therefore have to be made on who can obtain and who will be refused care and/or treatment.

The fact that there is no absolute duty to provide health care on demand means that waiting lists can be justified and that the courts accept that there is an uneven equation between the demands for health care and the resources to meet those demands. The two cases discussed in *Speller*, section 6.3.1, show the basis for this.

Read *Speller*, section 6.3.1, pp. 153-155, which sets out the statutory duty to provide health care and discusses the possibility of individual legal action. Then read section 2.1.1, pp. 18-20, studying carefully the statutory duties placed upon the Secretary of State by sections 1, 2 and 3 of the NHS Act 1977 given on p. 19.

As a result of the NHS and Community Care Act 1990, an internal market has been set up within the NHS. This means that the district health authorities as commissioners agree contracts for the provision of NHS services with providers who may or may not be NHS bodies. Group fund-holding practices are given a budget to purchase certain kinds of service from NHS and other bodies. This purchaser/provider divide has highlighted the dilemmas which arise and the decisions which have to be made. Where there is an NHS agreement which covers the provision of specified services in the locality, then the person resident within the jurisdiction of the district health authority is entitled to receive those services; this is unless the person is a patient attached to a group fund-holding practice, in which case he would look to that for the purchase of the necessary secondary and community services. Where the purchaser has not negotiated an agreement for certain services and a patient requires these services (e.g. regional services not provided in the catchment area or services from specialist hospitals outside the area), then the purchaser will have to give specific approval for the purchase of this service. This is known as an extra contractual referral (ECR).

ACTIVITY 31   ALLOW **20 MINUTES**

Having studied the statutory duties under the NHS Act 1977, answer the following questions:

1 Are there any patients whom you think should not be provided with treatment on the NHS? Consider, in particular, the following:

- smokers, in smoking-related cases

- attempted suicides

- drug and drink abusers

- the seriously obese

- those sustaining sports injuries: skiing, motor/cycle/horse racing, climbing, boxing, pot holing (on the grounds that they knew the risks of injury and voluntarily took them on)

- AIDS/HIV patients

- elderly people over 70 years

- those suffering from a persistent vegetative state

- those seeking a sex change

- those seeking a reversal of sterilisation

- those seeking cosmetic surgery.

Consider how you would defend any action for breach of statutory duty brought by a person who has been refused treatment.

2 What discretion should be left to the purchaser (i.e. the district health authority as commissioner of the services rather than provider) by the Secretary of State?

3 What provisions could be left out of the local NHS agreement between purchaser and provider?

4 Should the provision of ECRs be entirely dependent on financial resources being available? If not, what other criteria should determine whether ECRs are provided or refused?

5 Should the patient have a right of appeal if refused treatment under the questions above? If so, to whom? What mechanism should be set up?

6 What should be the role of the non-executive board member in determining these issues?

7 Should the patient under a fund-holding general practice have different rights to treatment and/or care than the patient whose general practitioner is not a fund-holder?

Commentary

These are difficult questions to answer, but given limited resources and an almost unlimited demand it is inevitable that some kind of rationing will have to take place. This could be in the form of deciding that certain services are not appropriate for the NHS to provide. For example, some districts have decided not to provide funds for cosmetic surgery or for the reversal of sterilisation operations. Controversy has been aroused by the announcement that surgery will not be offered to patients who smoke. There could be justification for this where smokers have an extremely bad prognosis with certain treatments.

Ultimately, since responsibility is with the Secretary of State, should any district fail to purchase services which she considers to be an integral part of health care, then she can direct the DHA to purchase the service. Thus, an Executive Letter (EL (90) MB115) was issued to ensure that family planning services continued to be provided within the NHS and charges were not made. However, since not all needs or demands can be met, health services need to devise mechanisms for determining priorities. From the legal point of view, if this decision-making is carried out rationally and is in accordance with the way in which any other health authority might have acted in the circumstances, then the courts will not intervene to challenge the decisions.

It is possible for a patient to bring an action for judicial review in the High Court of the Secretary of State's or health authority's decision. To date, litigants who have challenged the exercise of discretion and the priority setting of DHAs or the Secretary of State and alleged that there has been a breach of duty have not succeeded.

2: Statutory authorities

The authorities which have been established to carry out the functions of the Secretary of State are:

- district health authorities

- family health service authorities

- regional health authorities.

Read *Speller*, section 2.2, pp. 21-29, which covers the function and constitution of the statutory authorities. Note that the Secretary of State has issued plans to demolish regional health authorities in favour of agents reporting direct to the NHS Management Executive.

ACTIVITY 32   ALLOW 30 MINUTES

You have been asked to obtain a copy of the document, *Managing the New NHS: A Background Document* (DoH, 1993a) which sets out plans for the ending of regional health authorities and the new organisations which are to replace them. Read it and answer the following questions.

1   What are the advantages and disadvantages of having officers rather than members of a regional institution?

2   Do you consider that the health service requires an administrative layer between the district health authority and the Department of Health or Welsh Office or Scottish Office?

Commentary

An important reason for an interim administrative organisation between, on the one hand, the government departments and, on the other, the purchasing health authorities and NHS trusts is the danger that the span of control could become too large for effective management without an intermediary level. Much depends, however, on the extent of decentralisation and local decision-making. It may be that, in future, as a result of the amalgamation of commissioning authorities, there will be a few larger commissioning authorities at sub-regional levels.

Advisory machinery

Read *Speller*, section 2.3, pp. 29-33, which describes the advisory machinery at central and local level that was instituted to ensure that professionals working in the field are able to advise Government and the statutory authorities. Note in particular the Clinical Standards Advisory Group which was set up under section 62 of the 1990 Act.

The relationship between local authorities, health authorities and other bodies

Read through *Speller*, section 2.4, pp. 33-47, noting the following as you do so:

- the effect of section 22 of the NHS Act 1977

- the role of joint consultative committees

- the effect of section 28 and Schedule 8 of the NHS Act 1977.

The Government White Paper, *Caring for People: Community Care in the Next Decade* (1989), envisages a seamless service linking health and social services. Sections 22, 28 and Schedule 8 of the NHS Act 1977 are intended to make this possible. They cover the duty of the local authorities and the health authorities to work together in the provision of health and social care. At the heart of the relationship is the joint consultative committee (JCC) where officers at a senior level of both health and local authorities meet to consider the joint planning of services and agree allocations from the budget of one to the other. If you can create the opportunity to attend a JCC it would be useful for you to see this mechanism at work. Alternatively, if neither time nor the opportunity permits, you may be able to obtain sight of the papers for a JCC meeting.

Under section 23 of the 1977 Act, health services can be provided through voluntary and other bodies. Note that funds can be transferred under section 28A for the provision of community services.

Community health councils

Established in 1974 under the NHS Reorganisation Act 1973, community health councils (CHCs) have had a shaky existence and were under threat following the consultative paper, *Patients First* (DHSS and Welsh Office, 1979), which suggested that with local representatives on health authorities, CHCs may not have a clear role. However, they have survived and have been given important responsibilities in the consultation in relation to the changes in health service provision and the closure of hospitals. See, in particular, Regulations 18 and 19 of the Community Health Councils Regulations 1985 for the functions of the CHCs. Note, too, the powers they have to receive information under Regulation 20 to inspect premises under Regulation 21 and to have meetings with the DHAs under Regulation 22. Additional powers are given by the Community Health Councils (Access to Information) Act 1988, which enables them to attend certain meetings and to receive specified information.

ACTIVITY 33

ALLOW **10** MINUTES

Obtain a copy of the annual report of your local CHC. Look at:

● the membership

● its budget: income and expenditure

● its activities

● its business plan.

To what extent do you consider it is able to fulfil the functions set out in the 1977 Act and in the 1985 Regulations and what would you identify as the main constraints?

Commentary

You may well have been surprised to see how small a budget the CHC functions on. There are few funds for research activity and limited funds to obtain feedback from people in the area about the health services they are receiving. Note also that, apart from the Secretary to the CHC and his administrative support, there are few staff and the members provide their services voluntarily.

Internal arrangements

Read *Speller*, section 2.5, pp. 47-58, and make notes on the main points of interest to you.

Sections 85 and 86 of the NHS Act 1977 give the Secretary of State the power to declare that an authority is in default. Note the power of the Secretary of State under section 84 of the NHS Act 1977 and under section 125 of the Mental Health Act 1983 to set up an inquiry. Witnesses can be compelled to attend and give evidence; the production of documents can also be enforced.

Note the protection that members and officers of health authorities and trusts receive in the performance of their duties under section 265 of the Public Health Act 1875, now incorporated into the NHS Act 1977 and the 1990 NHS and Community Care Act.

Purchasers/providers and the internal market

Reference has already been made to the fact that the 1990 Act set up the framework to enable the internal market to be created. Eventually very few health services will be provided by health authorities as direct labour services; the vast majority of services will be provided through NHS trusts. These will agree NHS contracts with purchasers, who may be health authorities or GP fund-holding practices.

Note that the intention of part of section 4 of the 1990 Act is to prevent litigation in court between purchaser and provider over an NHS agreement. Instead, if there are serious disagreements between purchasers and providers, then the Act provides for a dispute machinery which was set up under Statutory Instrument (1991) No. 725 National Health Service Contracts (Dispute Resolution) Regulations.

3: NHS trusts

Read carefully *Speller*, **section 2.6, pp. 58-70, which sets out the workings of the NHS trusts.**

ACTIVITY 34
ALLOW 30 MINUTES

Obtain and read or look through a copy of the following:

- the NHS trust application for your local hospital (or the nearest hospital which has made a successful application for trust status)

- the NHS contract between a purchaser and provider for the trust; (this might be kept secret and you may have to ask for sight of it in a particular place and agree to keep the information confidential)

- the annual report of the trust

- any documents which the CHC has prepared on the local situation.

If you work in the non-NHS sector, try to obtain comparable documents about your own employer.

Identify a specific aspect of the service which interests you (e.g. maternity services or mental health provision) and analyse the terms of the agreement in relation to quantity and quality. Identify the standards which are set and decide what would be appropriate monitoring tools.

Contrast the present situation with the arrangements prevailing before the 1990 Act was implemented, when there was no clear purchaser/provider split. To what extent do you consider that patients benefit from the introduction of the internal market?

Commentary

In your analysis of your chosen area of provision, you should have been able to identify the size of service provision in terms of in-patient days or numbers of operations, etc. You should also have been able to identify quality standards and how the purchasers intended to monitor contract performance.

One of the effects of the introduction of the internal market is the sharper costings of individual patient care and the clearer picture which is now available of comparative hospital costs. This information is likely to lead to league tables being used to compare services both in terms of cost and in terms of success across the country and across the NHS/non-NHS divide.

4: Handling complaints in the health service

Chapter 8 of *Speller* covers the statutory duty placed upon the health service to provide a complaints procedure. It also covers the function of the Health Service Commissioner and his jurisdiction. Mention is made of the power of the Secretary of State to initiate an inquiry into any matter which he deems advisable under section 84 of the National Health Service Act 1977. The role of the Mental Health Act Commission is considered in *Speller*, chapter 30, section 30.12; it is also discussed briefly in the last section of this session.

Read through *Speller*, section 8.1, pp. 291-301, and look for the essential features required by the government guidance. Then undertake the following activity.

ACTIVITY 35 — ALLOW 30 MINUTES

Compare the procedure for handling a non-clinical complaint with that for a clinical complaint. If possible obtain a copy of the complaints procedure of your local hospital. Draw a diagram so that the contrast between the clinical and the non-clinical procedures can be easily compared; this might also be a useful guide for the general public or new employees.

Ask to see the annual report on complaints which your hospital or trust has prepared. This should show the type of complaint, the time it takes for them to be resolved and the outcome. Are there any surprises?

Commentary

You will probably have noticed that the statutory provisions only apply to hospital complaints; thus, complaints relating to community health services are not covered. The Department of Health guidance suggests that a similar procedure should be drawn up for the community health services. In addition, the Patients' Charter requires there to be a complaints procedure for all health care and requires each district and NHS trust to draw up its own procedure based on the general principles.

Under section 50 of the NHS and Community Care Act 1990, the Secretary of State is given powers to require local authorities to prepare procedures for handling complaints. Directions were issued on the basis of this power (SI 1990 No. 2244). You should be able to obtain a copy of the procedure of your own local authority which you can compare with the one for your hospital.

In May 1994 the report by the committee set up by the Department of Health and chaired by Professor Alan Wilson was published, *Being Heard: The Report of a Review Committee on NHS Complaints Procedures* (DoH, 1994). It invited consultation on a streamlined procedure covering both hospital complaints and those arising in the community and against general practitioners. It recommended that a three-stage complaint procedure should be set up on the basis of nine principles: responsiveness, quality enhancement, cost-effectiveness, accessibility, impartiality, simplicity, speed, confidentiality and accountability. At present the Department of Health's reaction to responses from the consultation exercise is awaited, as are any directions relating to the establishment of a new procedure across the health services. Look out for the publication of any changes.

The Health Service Commissioner

The post of Health Service Commissioner (also known as the Ombudsman) was established in 1974. The duties, powers and jurisdiction of the Commissioner are set out in Part V of the National Health Service Act 1977 and in Schedule 13 of that Act.

Read *Speller*, section 8.4, pp. 302-315, and make notes on:

- the circumstances in which the Commissioner is authorised to investigate

- the matters or circumstances which are outside his jurisdiction.

  Note the distinction between clinical and non-clinical matters and the examples given in the text where clinical matters may come within the jurisdiction of the Commissioner.

The Commissioner provides an annual report of his activities and also prepares summaries of selected cases. His report is presented to the Parliamentary Select Committee on the Health Service Commissioner. This Committee is able to investigate cases further by requiring relevant persons, including the managers and senior medical staff, to be called to give evidence to the Select Committee. Their findings are then reported. Whilst the Commissioner has no power to require sanctions from health service bodies or employees if a complaint is upheld, the possibility that non-compliance with any of his suggestions could lead to further inquiries by the Select Committee is a powerful tool in compelling a recalcitrant authority to comply with the Commissioner's suggestions in making amends.

ACTIVITY 36   ALLOW 20 MINUTES

Analyse the following situations and decide if the Commissioner can investigate:

1 A member of staff complains that certain patients in a geriatric ward are being cruelly treated by a volunteer on the ward.

2 A patient complains that the wrong leg was amputated and the hospital have denied liability.

3 The mother of a child complains that the regime on the children's ward with early waking, inedible food and over-discipline of the children is too harsh. Since, however, her child has a chronic condition, she does not wish to complain to the managers personally.

4 A woman who has had both breasts removed following a diagnosis of cancer, complains that she was never given the choice of alternative treatments to surgery such as chemotherapy or radiotherapy.

5 Some staff complain that the rates of pay for health care assistants are so low that sufficiently high quality recruits are not being attracted and patient safety is therefore endangered.

6 The relative of a deceased patient complains that he should not have been removed from intensive care only two days before his death and had he remained in intensive care he would not have died. The managers have responded to his complaint by stating that beds were required in intensive care for patients with higher priorities.

7 A patient registered with a general practitioner complains that there is no appointments system in his surgery and consequently patients have to wait for an unacceptably long time.

8 The parents of a baby who died from an infection following surgery are not satisfied that the standards of cleanliness and cross-infection control are adequate and they remain dissatisfied with the hospital's response.

9 A mentally disordered patient complains that he is being given compulsory treatment without compliance with the provisions of the Mental Health Act 1983.

Commentary

1 This complaint is within the jurisdiction of the Commissioner but he would want to see the result of the NHS trust's investigation into the complaint before he commenced his own investigation.

2 This is a case where there is a clear cause of action in the civil courts and the Commissioner would ascertain the intention of the complainant before investigating himself. On the facts, his jurisdiction is unlikely to be excluded on the basis of clinical judgement.

3 As for question 1. The Commissioner should be able to obtain an undertaking of no victimisation.

4 This is likely to be excluded from the jurisdiction of the Commissioner on the grounds of clinical judgement.

5 Staff matters are excluded from the jurisdiction of the Commissioner.

6 The decision-making in this case appears to be on the basis of administrative procedures rather than clinical judgement and the Commissioner could make a preliminary investigation to see if this is so.

7 This is not within the jurisdiction of the Commissioner since complaints relating to doctors, dentists and pharmacists (services contracted with the FHSA) are outside his jurisdiction. He can, however, investigate how the FHSA handles these complaints.

8 This is within the jurisdiction of the Commissioner.

9 This would normally be referred to the Mental Health Act Commission who has the jurisdiction to investigate complaints relating to detained patients (see below).

5: Complaints relating to the Mental Health Act 1983

The Mental Health Act Commission has a statutory duty to handle complaints from detained patients. The subject of mentally disordered patients will be considered in detail in Session Eight, but here we will look briefly at the jurisdiction and function of the Mental Health Act Commission.

Read *Speller*, section 30.12, pp. 844-847.

The two distinct circumstances in which the Mental Health Act Commission (MHAC) can investigate complaints are covered by sections 120(1)(b)(i) and 120(1)(b)(ii) of the Act. Under section 120(2), the arrangements in respect of the investigation of complaints 'shall not require any person exercising functions under the arrangements to undertake or continue with any investigation where he does not consider it appropriate to do so.' This means that the Mental Health Act Commission, to whom has been delegated the task of investigating complaints by the Secretary of State, has discretion over investigating complaints.

ACTIVITY 37 — ALLOW 10 MINUTES

Note the contrasts between the jurisdiction of the Mental Health Act Commission and the Health Service Commissioner in the investigation of complaints. Return to the notes you made on the jurisdiction of the Health Service Commissioner and contrast it with that of the Mental Health Act Commission under section 120 of the Mental Health Act 1983.

Commentary

You will have seen that on the one hand the jurisdiction of the Mental Health Act Commission is much narrower in that it only relates to complaints from a detained patient or in relation to the Mental Health Act powers and duties. However, the jurisdiction does not exclude clinical matters and therefore the Mental Health Act Commission is able to investigate complaints relating to clinical judgement on treatment and care. It can also investigate cases where there are alternative remedies. However, the Mental Health Act Commission in its role as investigator of complaints and other matters is itself subject to investigation by the Health Service Commissioner. In 1993 the Commissioner investigated a complaint relating to the Mental Health Act Commission and the results of the investigation can be seen in the *Fifth Biennial Report (1991-1993) of the Mental Health Act Commission* (MHAC, 1993).

Summary

- There is no absolute duty on the Secretary of State to provide health care in all circumstances, so decisions have to be made about when treatment or care is withheld.

- The introduction of the internal market has changed the way the NHS operates, and further changes in the administrative structure are planned.

- Machinery is in place to regulate relationships with the health services.

- There are procedures for dealing with complaints in hospital.

- The Health Service Commissioner is empowered to investigate complaints of a non-clinical nature and report to the Parliamentary Select Committee on the Health Service Commissioner.

- The Mental Health Act Commission has a statutory duty to pursue complaints from or on behalf of detained patients and is not restricted to non-clinical matters.

Before you move onto Session Seven, check that you have achieved the objectives given at the beginning of this session and, if not, review the appropriate sections.

SESSION SEVEN

Legal issues relating to property

Introduction

This session looks at issues of liability in relation to the loss or damage of property. It is concerned not only with the protection of property belonging to the patient and his visitors, but it also looks at the problems of the employer in relation to the theft and damage of property belonging to the authority, and its powers in relation to the search and arrest and control of staff.

Session objectives

When you have completed this session, you should be able to:

- discuss the legal principles which relate to the protection of personal property

- debate the need for procedures to secure patient property on health services premises

- explain the law relating to the preparation and execution of wills in relation to patients

- summarise the powers and limitations of the managers' ability to search for stolen property and the rights of a citizen to effect an arrest.

1: The property of patients and visitors

Duty of care from the bailment of goods

Two different situations must be distinguished:

- where a health authority, trust or employee accepts responsibility for the property of another

- where property is brought onto the premises of the health service body for which no liability is assumed, although there may be liability under the Occupier's Liability Act 1957.

In the first circumstances there is a duty of care arising from the bailment of goods. In this case the health authority or the person assuming responsibility for the property is known as the bailee, and the person who entrusted the property to the bailee is known as the bailor. Should the property be lost or damaged during the bailment (i.e. the time during which the bailee is responsible for it), the onus is on the bailee to show that what occurred was without any negligence on his part.

In the second situation, in the absence of any particular circumstances such as where a patient is unconscious, there is no assumption of liability by the health authority or occupier.

Read *Speller*, Chapter 10, pp. 332-339.

ACTIVITY 38   ALLOW 15 MINUTES

Consider the following situations and decide if there is a duty of care owed by the hospital employees or others.

1 An unconscious patient is brought into hospital. A search of his pockets shows that he is carrying over £500 in cash.

2 A patient is admitted onto the ward and advised to hand over any valuables to the ward officer. She refuses since she claims that she has never been parted from her jewellery: a bracelet, necklace and several rings.

3 A patient attends for an X-ray and is asked to take off his clothes apart from his underwear and leave them in the cubicle whilst he is X-rayed.

4 A patient dies on the ward. In her locker is a purse and several items of jewellery.

5 An elderly person in the community is brought in to hospital under section 47 of the National Assistance Act 1948. She lived on her own and did not appear to have any relatives or friends.

6 A psychiatric nurse comes to work at the hospital on a motor bike. It is missing at the end of his shift although he had left it securely locked. It is subsequently discovered that an informal patient had made off with it and caused considerable damage to it. The member of staff did not have insurance cover for theft.

7 A member of staff accepts a watch from a patient to keep secure until the patient returns from the operating theatre.

8 A doctor on call who uses hospital accommodation left his passport, cheque card and cheque book in his hospital bedroom and they are stolen.

Commentary

1 Even though there has been no handing over of property to the hospital for safe-keeping, in these circumstances the hospital would become an involuntary bailee for the £500 in cash found on the unconscious patient. There should be a procedure for witnessing the taking of property from the patient and its safe custody. The patient should be told of this action as soon as he is capable of understanding what has happened, and be told that the property can be restored to him when he so wishes. Difficulties have sometimes arisen because the hospital would bank such cash and if the patient does not have a bank account he is likely to be unwilling to accept a cheque for the funds on discharge from hospital. Appropriate arrangements should be made so that the patient can either have the cash restored or be offered facilities to cash a cheque.

2 When the patient refuses to hand over the property she should be advised, preferably in writing as well as by word of mouth, that the hospital cannot accept responsibility for the property unless it is handed over to it for safe-keeping. A notice exempting the hospital from liability in such circumstances may be effective depending upon the reasonableness of reliance upon this notice.

3 The staff should ensure that the patient is asked to bring his clothes with him, unless a locker can be provided or the cubicle locked. Failure of the staff to take appropriate precautions may lead to the hospital board being liable.

4 If a patient becomes unconscious or dies, the hospital staff have a duty of care to take responsibility for the property in the locker or in the ward. Arrangements should be made for an inventory to be carried out. If the patient dies, the hospital would hold any property on trust for the personal representatives or executors of the estate.

5 Under section 48 of the National Assistance Act 1947, the local authority has a responsibility to take care of the property of any patient who is moved to hospital or a place of safety. There should be liaison between the hospital personnel and the social services department over the care of the property once the patient is removed.

6 Staff, like patients, bring property onto hospital premises at their own risk. In this case, even though the property has been taken by an informal patient, it is unlikely that the hospital managers would be regarded as being responsible for the patient's actions. There is unlikely to be any liability for this theft.

7 In this case, the member of staff has become the bailee of the watch. It is his duty to ensure that it is returned safely to the patient when he has recovered from the operation.

8 Hospitals are not liable for the safety of property in staff rooms. If it is subsequently discovered that the property was stolen by a member of staff, the doctor might find it difficult to establish that the employee was acting in the course of employment when he stole the property, and thus he might be unable to hold the employers vicariously liable for the theft.

If you are not clear about these issues, re-read the cases of *Martin v. London County Council* 1947 and *Edwards v. West Herts Group HMC* 1957 in sections 10.1 and 10.2 of *Speller,* and ensure that you understand why in the one case the hospital was held liable and in the other not.

Disclaiming responsibility for property

The duty of care can be disclaimed if it is reasonable so to do. Section 10.2 of *Speller* sets out the provisions for disclaiming responsibility for property. To be effective, the disclaimer notice must be brought to the attention of the patient or visitor and it must be reasonable for the person seeking to avoid liability to rely upon it. In this situation, the Unfair Contract Terms Act 1977 would apply. The relevant sections are set out below:

'2.   Negligence liability.– (1) A person cannot by reference to any contract term or to a notice given to persons generally or to particular persons exclude or restrict his liability for death or personal injury resulting from negligence.

(2) In the case of other loss or damage, a person cannot so exclude or restrict his liability for negligence except in so far as the term or notice satisfies the requirement of reasonableness.

(3) Where a contract term or notice purports to exclude or restrict liability for negligence a person's agreement to or awareness of it is not of itself to be taken as indicating his voluntary acceptance of any risk.'

'11.   The 'reasonableness' test.– (1) In relation to a contract term, the requirement of reasonableness for the purposes of this Part of this Act . . . is that the term shall have been a fair and reasonable one to be included having regard to the circumstances which were, or ought reasonably to have been, known to or in the contemplation of the parties when the contract was made.'

'(3) In relation to a notice (not being a notice having contractual effect), the requirement of reasonableness under this Act is that it should be fair and reasonable to allow reliance on it, having regard to all the circumstances obtaining when the liability arose or (but for the notice) would have arisen.

(4) Where by reference to a contract term or notice a person seeks to restrict liability to a specified sum of money, and the question arises (under this or any other Act) whether the term or notice satisfies the requirement of reasonableness, regard shall be had in particular . . . to:–

(a) the resources which he could expect to be available to him for the purpose of meeting the liability should it arise; and

(b) how far it was open to him to cover himself by insurance.

(5) It is for those claiming that a contract term or notice satisfies the requirement of reasonableness to show that it does.'

Notice is defined in the Act as including 'an announcement, whether or not in writing, and any other communication or pretended communication' (Section 14).

ACTIVITY 39   ALLOW **10** MINUTES

A visitor parks her car in the parking area of a district general hospital. She buys a parking ticket at the kiosk and attaches it to the windscreen inside the car. A large notice is displayed by the pay kiosk which disclaims any liability for cars parked in the area. It states 'The YE trust is not liable for any loss or damage to vehicles parked in this area however caused.' Two hours later, when she returns to the car, she discovers that there is a large dent in the side with many scratches and the paintwork severely damaged. A piece of paper is attached to the windscreen. This states that a witness saw the car damaged by a hospital vehicle and gives the registration number and is prepared to give evidence to this effect should it be necessary. The visitor seeks compensation from the YE NHS trust, but the latter, in reliance on the notice, refuses to pay any compensation, holding that it has effectively disclaimed liability.

Analyse the law relating to this situation referring to the Unfair Contract Terms Act 1977 given above. Is the visitor likely to win her claim for compensation?

Commentary

This activity requires you to apply the Unfair Contract Terms Act to the situation and, in particular, to determine the reasonableness of the trust in relying upon the notice to exclude liability for the negligence of its staff. It must be remembered that, where the exemption clause is relied upon, it is for the party relying upon it to show the reasonableness of the exemption. Any doubts on this should therefore be resolved in favour of the visitor.

More details relating to the exact circumstances would be necessary in order to give a clear answer on the visitor's likely success: how was her car parked; were there parking lines; was the hospital vehicle being driven in a dangerous, as opposed to careless, manner; is it fair and reasonable for the trust to rely on the exemption? She may well have a very good chance of succeeding against the trust, and the trust may be prepared to make an *ex gratia* payment to avoid adverse publicity and inconvenience.

ACTIVITY 40   ALLOW 30 MINUTES

Obtain a copy of the procedure laid down by your hospital or other premises in relation to the property of patients and staff, and consider the extent to which it would provide protection for the health service body in the event that, for instance, the property given in the examples in Activity 38 is lost or damaged.

If your workplace does not have such a procedure, draft a suitable policy for staff and patients.

Commentary

Features you should look for are:

1 A clear setting out of the legal situation.

2 The hospital (or relevant authority) not taking responsibility for any property other than that specifically left in the custody and care of a member of staff. The arrangements for so doing should be set out.

3 Warnings for patients not to bring valuable property into hospital with them and making it clear that the hospital (or relevant authority) will not be liable for any loss or damage to such property.

4   The situation in relation to property brought onto hospital (or other) premises by the staff.

5   The arrangements for the circulation of the procedures to both staff and patients.

2: Making a will

Read *Speller*, **Chapter 26, pp. 680-685.**

If a patient wishes to make a will in hospital, every opportunity should be given for this to be done. Whenever possible the patient should be encouraged to obtain the services of his own solicitor in the drawing up of the will. This is because a will can be challenged on the grounds of:

- its failure to comply with the formalities required by Act of Parliament

- the patient being mentally incapable of making a will

- the mind of the testator (i.e. the person making the will) being under the undue influence of another person and therefore the disposition of the property not reflecting the real intentions of the testator.

Requirements for the validity of a will are set out in Section 9 of the Wills Act 1837 as amended by the Administration of Justice Act 1982. This states that:

- the testator must be of sound mind and of full age

- the will must be in writing and signed by the testator (or by some other person in his presence and by his directions)

- the testator must have intended by his signature to give effect to the will

- the signature is made or acknowledged by the testator in the presence of two or more witnesses present at the same time who either attest and sign the will or acknowledge his signature in the presence of the testator, but not necessarily in the presence of any other witness

- no form of attestation shall be necessary; i.e. the Act does not require a specific form to be completed or a particular way in which the signatures are given.

Note the case of *Re Colling, deceased* (1972) and the result that the will was declared to be invalid.

Patients of unsound mind

Note the definition given in the *Harwood v. Baker* case of a sound mind for the purpose of making a will. If it is clear that a person who wishes to dispose of his property lacks the capacity to make a will, then the Court of Protection has the power to execute a will on his behalf. The powers are given in section 96 of the Mental Health Act 1983 and discussed in section 26.3.2 of *Speller*.

Where the patient wishes to make a will and there is a doubt about the mental capacity of the patient, it is advisable to seek the opinion of the doctor in charge of the patient on the patient's mental competence to understand what he is doing.

Where a will is challenged on the basis that the testator was under the influence of another person when he made the will so that the will does not give effect to his real intentions, the challenger would have to show that there is evidence of undue influence, that the testator was under this influence and that he would have made different provisions had this influence not been present. The success of the challenge will depend entirely upon the facts which can be proved. The involvement of a solicitor in the execution of the will can assist in preventing any undue influence being brought to bear by another person.

ACTIVITY 41
ALLOW 30 MINUTES

Draw up a procedure for staff that would be effective in both a hospital and a community setting in the event of a patient wishing to make a will. It should include reference to patients suffering from mental disorder and guidance to staff in relation to the significance of the mental competence of the person wishing to make a will. Then, using an imaginary situation, consider the extent to which your draft would cover all reasonably foreseeable events.

Commentary

It may well be that your employer has already prepared such a procedure. If so, compare your draft with this. If not, check your draft against the guidelines on the validity of wills given above and in *Speller*. Note that it should advise staff that it is preferable for the patient to obtain the professional help of a solicitor.

Property of patients who are mentally disordered

In this unit we are not dealing with the constitution and functions of the Court of Protection, which takes care of the property of patients with mental disorder. If you have a particular interest in this area you should study *Speller*, pp. 855–858, section 30.18.

3: Search and arrest

Theft of health service property is a growing problem that is shared with many other organisations which face the possibility of losses from property stolen from their premises. Sometimes staff are responsible and it is essential that employers and managers are aware of the law relating to searching for stolen property and arresting those suspected of stealing. Chapter 12 of *Speller* sets out the law relating to search and arrest.

Search

The safest course to pursue is to assume that the employer or manager does not have the power in law to search another person or his property without his consent. Even where a clause is included in the contract of employment which gives the employer the right to search a member of staff or his possessions, it is advisable for the employer not to force this in the event of the employee refusing to allow the search. The employer could, in the event of that refusal, consider the case to be one of breach of contract and therefore a matter for disciplinary procedure. Even former police officers employed as security staff do not possess any powers greater than those of the citizen.

What of the situation where it is feared that mentally disordered patients may bring onto the premises dangerous weapons, matches or other forbidden objects? In this situation guidance is provided by the *Mental Health Act Code of Practice* (DoH, 1993b) issued by the Department of Health initially in 1990 and revised in 1993. See *Speller* p. 345, section 12.2.

Note the limitations upon the occupier's or employer's right to search the residential quarters of staff or the lockers of staff and patients. A line is drawn between entry into staff residences for the purpose of housekeeping or the cleaning of lockers and the deliberate searching of such rooms or furniture.

Arrest

Power is given by statute for a citizen's arrest in two different circumstances:

1   Where an arrestable offence is being committed or there is reasonable belief that one is being committed.

    See section 24(4) of the Police and Criminal Evidence Act 1984 which is set out on p. 347 of *Speller*. There are considerable dangers in making use of this power since, if it turned out that an arrestable offence was not being committed, then the person making the arrest would have acted unlawfully and be liable to the charge of false imprisonment, unless he had reasonable grounds for suspecting that such an offence was being committed.

2   Where an arrestable offence has been committed.

    See section 24(5) set out in *Speller*, p. 348. Again, if there is subsequently shown to be no arrestable offence, then the person arresting will be guilty of false imprisonment.

In the light of this statutory protection in arrests by the private citizen, it is far preferable to make use of the powers of the police by bringing them into the organisation at the appropriate time.

ACTIVITY 42   ALLOW 15 MINUTES

> After a bout of severe losses from the kitchen stores, the unit manager and catering officer decide to mount a watch to find out who is stealing. They hide themselves and then, when certain staff are leaving work, they surprise them, taking away their handbags and other shopping bags. The staff refuse to give consent but their protests are ignored. The staff are taken into the manager's office and kept there for two hours until the police arrive. The search, however, proves fruitless and no stolen goods are discovered. The staff are now suing the NHS trust for compensation for false imprisonment. The trust is relying upon the protection provided by the Police and Criminal Evidence Act 1984.
>
> What are the strengths and weaknesses of the claim by the staff and who do you think will win any litigation?

Commentary

To answer this question, it is necessary to apply section 24(4) and (5) of the Police and Criminal Evidence Act 1984 to the circumstances. Since no stolen property was found, it will be difficult, if not impossible, to establish that an arrestable offence had been or was being committed. In this event, the employees might have a successful case of wrongful arrest, i.e. false imprisonment, and also of trespass to property in the taking of their bags and the search which took place. Had stolen property been found, the actions of the managers may well have been protected by the Police and Criminal Evidence Act 1984.

Summary

- When the hospital, other authority or its employee becomes the bailee, even if involuntarily, it/he is responsible for the property. In other circumstances there is no assumption of liability.

- The duty of care can be disclaimed if it is reasonable to do so, in which case the disclaimer should be brought to the attention of the patient, visitor or member of staff to be relied upon.

- Patients should be given every opportunity to make a will if they wish to do so, but if there is any doubt about their mental capacity it is advisable to seek the doctor's opinion.

- A manager effecting a citizen's arrest without a reasonable belief that an offence is being or has been committed, might be guilty of false imprisonment.

- It is advisable to obtain the person's consent before searching them or their property.

Before moving on to Session Eight, check that you have achieved the objectives given at the beginning of this session. If not, review the relevant sections.

Mental health law

Introduction

This session considers the law relating to the treatment and care of mentally disordered patients. The law is mainly contained in the Mental Health Act 1983 which has 10 parts, not all of which are covered in this session. Each part is divided into sections. Chapter 30 of *Speller* covers a wider range of topics than we will be looking at in this unit. However, topics such as the provisions for criminal offenders (Part III), the role and function of the court of protection (Part VII) and of the mental health review tribunals (Part V) are important. They are given a full treatment in *Speller* and you are encouraged to study them when you have the opportunity.

The areas we will be covering in this session are:

- the formal admission of a patient under Part II of the Mental Health Act 1983

- leave of absence from hospital under section 17 and the retaking of patients under section 18 of the same Act

- guardianship

- discharge of patients, managers' review and managers' duties

- medical treatment for detained patients.

It is strongly recommended that you obtain a copy of the Mental Health Act 1983 and the revised *Mental Health Act Code of Practice* prepared by the Department of Health (DoH, 1993b).

Session objectives

At the end of this session, you should be able to:

- describe in what circumstances persons can be detained against their will in a psychiatric hospital or mental nursing home registered to take detained patients

- specify the laws relating to the granting of leave of absence to detained patients and the retaking of detained patients

- explain the principles relating to guardianship orders and their role within the context of care in the community

- discuss the role of managers in reviewing the detention of patients

- summarise provisions relating to the giving of compulsory treatment for mental disorder and the protection of the patient.

1: Compulsory admission for mental disorder

The loss of an individual's freedom on the grounds of mental disorder must be closely controlled; that is why the Mental Health Act 1983 is so significant to the rights of the patient. It prevents a person from being unjustifiably detained and provides protection for the patient to challenge decisions relating to his detention at specific intervals. The Act also places a duty upon the managers of a hospital or nursing home where a patient is detained to ensure that there is an application at set intervals to a mental health review tribunal in case the patient or his nearest relative through ignorance, apathy or disorder have not applied themselves.

The sections of the Act which permit detention of a patient are:

- section 5(2) and section 5(4) for detention of an informal patient

- sections 4 and 2 for admission for assessment

- section 3 for admission for treatment.

In the case of sections 2, 3 and 4, the applicant must be either an approved social worker or the nearest relative of the patient. For sections 2 and 3 there must be two medical recommendations both stating the same mental disorder (whether or not they mention another); for section 4, which permits admission in an emergency situation, there need only be one medical recommendation. Note the definition of nearest relative given in *Speller*.

Read *Speller*, sections 30.4.1-30.4.11, pp. 736-757.

ACTIVITY 43   ALLOW 30 MINUTES

With reference to the Mental Health Act 1983 and to the sections of *Speller* you have just read, prepare a chart showing the following information for each of sections 2, 3 and 4:

- the section number

- the maximum duration of the section without renewal

- the number of medical recommendations required

- the nature of mental disorder which must be present

- the applicant.

Commentary

MIND has prepared a chart showing this information which you might like to obtain.

Note that the duration of all the sections should be stated as 'up to' the maximum time, since the responsible medical officer can discharge from a section any patient at any time if he considers that the statutory requirements are no longer met. In addition, as we shall see, the hospital managers can hear appeals against detention and have the power to discharge the patient from a section.

Section 2

Note that whilst this is called 'admission for assessment', the Act explicitly permits patients to be given treatment under compulsion if necessary whilst under this section. This is further discussed below.

Section 4

All the statutory requirements for section 2 must be present for this section to be used, other than the requirement to have the medical recommendations of two doctors. The criteria for an emergency situation must exist.

Section 3

This would normally be used for a patient who had already been assessed and provides for admission to hospital for treatment. Note the paragraphs from the statutory Code of Practice (DoH, 1993b) quoted on pp. 756-757 of *Speller* which set out when section 2 or when section 3 is appropriate.

Make sure you are clear about the distinction between section 2 and section 3 regarding the nearest relative. This person must be consulted under section 3, but can be merely informed under section 2 (see *Speller*, p. 740 and p. 748). In extreme circumstances, consideration may have to be given to the replacement of the nearest relative under section 29(c) of the Mental Health Act 1983: i.e. where the nearest relative unreasonably objects to the making of an application for admission for treatment (*Speller*, p. 748).

2: Leave of absence

Read *Speller*, sections 30.4.16 and 30.4.17, pp. 766-770.

Leave of absence is a useful stage within the treatment plan of the detained patient, as the recovery progresses. Section 17 of the Mental Health Act 1983 regulates it tightly in that it can only be granted by the responsible medical officer. The revised Code of Practice has provided further guidance on the implementation of section 17. Leave of absence can be ended at any time if the responsible medical officer is of the view 'that it is necessary so to do in the interests of the patient's health or safety or for the protection of other persons'. He then gives written notice of that fact to the patient or to the person in charge of the patient and revokes the leave of absence.

If a patient fails to return after the leave of absence has been revoked or if the patient leaves the hospital without obtaining approval, then section 18 permits the patient to be returned to custody by any approved social worker, by any officer on the staff of the hospital, by any police officer or by any person authorised in writing by the managers of the hospital.

Note the details of the Hallstrom case, which effectively prevented doctors using detention under the Mental Health Act 1983 as a 'long leash'; i.e. the patient was placed under section, immediately discharged into the community under threat that if she failed to take her medication she would be brought back into the institution, and she was returned to the hospital in time for the renewal of the section. The courts declared this practice illegal.

ACTIVITY 44   ALLOW **20** MINUTES

The Code of Practice recommends that the granting of leave of absence to a patient under section 17 should be put in writing and a form should be specifically designed for the task.

Draft a form which can be completed by the responsible medical officer which gives approval to leave of absence on specific occasions. The form should contain all the relevant details of the patient and be sufficiently clear for nursing staff to administer. It should also warn the nursing staff of any contra-indications.

Commentary

Your form should have the following details:

- full name of patient

- ward/department the patient is on

- section details of patient:

  - section number

  - date of commencement

  - date of expiry

- details of leave:

  - the nature of the approved leave of absence: e.g. weekend leave, twice weekly visits to shops, etc.

  - whether or not the leave is escorted or unescorted

  - over what period of time the approval runs

- any factors which would prevent leave being given

- any additional information or action required before leave is taken, e.g. in relation to medication

- full name of the responsible medical officer granting leave

- the signature of the responsible medical officer

- the date.

3: Guardianship and care in the community

Section 7 of the Act sets out the provisions relating to an application for guardianship. Exactly the same requirements are necessary as for an application under section 3, except that the patient is not required to be detained in hospital.

Section 8 gives the powers of the guardian which replaced the powers under the 1959 Act.

Read *Speller*, section 30.4.18, pp. 770-773, and section 30.20.2, pp. 868-869.

Section 117 of the Act requires the health authority and the local authority to link with other organisations in providing after-care services for a patient who has been detained under sections 3 or 37, or transferred under sections 47 or 48. Some authorities have integrated provisions for section 117 within the Care Programme Approach. However, since there are clear, enforceable statutory duties imposed by section 117, it would seem wiser for the duties covered by it to be recorded and administered separately. The duties under section 117 last until both authorities are satisfied that the person concerned is no longer in need of such services.

ACTIVITY 45   ALLOW 90 MINUTES

Considerable discussion has taken place recently over the need for a community supervision order. This has been provoked by evidence that patients, often those who have had frequent spells of admission in hospital, are not getting sufficient supervision to prevent the need for readmission. Reports have been prepared by the Royal College of Psychiatrists (1993), by the Health Committee of the House of Commons (1993) and by an internal review committee set up by the Department of Health (DoH, 1993c).

Read the reports of the Health Committee (1993) and the internal review committee (DoH, 1993c) that you have been asked to obtain and write notes on the following:

1 What is the problem?

2 What solutions are being proposed?

3 Why is the strengthening of guardianship not the answer?

4 What do you consider are the best ways of meeting the problem?

Commentary

By the time you are studying this unit it might be that legislation has been passed to implement the findings of the internal review report. If so, obtain a copy of the new Act and compare it with the recommendations in the reports.

The problem is the so-called revolving door phenomenon, where long-term chronic patients are unable to stay on a treatment regime which enables them to remain in the community. The reasons might be social and economic; they might also be medical since medication does not necessarily resolve all the medical problems.

Suggestions for solutions vary. Some recommend there should be the power to force patients to have treatment whilst still in the community rather than return them to the institution for compulsory treatment to be given. Others have argued that no additional legal powers are required provided guardianship is used effectively and the necessary resources are made available to enable these people to remain in the community. In some ways the community supervision order would work on a pre-Hallstrom basis, i.e. the patient remains in the community, but can be transferred back into custodial care when necessary, subject to some safeguards for him to challenge the return to hospital.

4: Discharge of patients and the duties of managers

Read *Speller*, section 30.4.20, p. 776.

Section 23 of the Mental Health Act 1983 enables the detained patient to appeal to the managers for discharge. This right is in addition to the right to appeal to a mental health review tribunal at specified intervals. (We will not be considering mental health review tribunals in this unit, but you can find them discussed in *Speller*, pp. 823-839, section 30.8.) The managers are defined in section 23(4) of the Mental Health Act 1983 which does not permit this power of discharge to be delegated to officers. NHS trusts are able to use co-opted members for the hearing of appeals as a result of the Mental Health (Amendment) Act 1994, which came into force on 14 April 1994. There are no specific formalities which the managers must follow in hearing an appeal. They should apply the principles of natural justice, however, by allowing each party to have the opportunity of speaking or being represented, and any manager with an interest should disqualify himself from sitting on the appeal.

ACTIVITY 46   ALLOW 30 MINUTES

Referring to the section of *Speller* you have just read, and the booklet, *Hearing Patients' Appeals Against Continued Compulsory Detention* (Williamson, 1991), prepare a procedure to be followed by managers in the hearing of appeals by detained patients. Your procedure should cover the information required in advance and the process to be followed during the hearing, including the location, the hearing of the witnesses and the substantive law that they are obliged to follow. It should also include the action to be taken after the hearing.

Commentary

Pre-hearing

The procedure should list the reports required in advance of the hearing, such as those from the responsible medical officer, social worker, nurse and others. The reports should clearly identify any information which the writer considers would cause serious harm to the physical or mental health of the patient if disclosed to him. The timing for receipt in relation to the hearing date should also be specified.

Hearing

The procedure should set out in full the relevant sections of the Act which give grounds for detention (e.g. section 2(2) and section 3(2)) and the grounds for the renewal under section 20 which the managers must be satisfied exist. The managers must apply these criteria for detention or renewal to the facts they see before them. The procedure must ensure that at least three managers are present to hear the appeal.

Post-hearing

The decision of the managers should be recorded in writing. The procedure should specify how and by whom the patient and staff are to be notified of the decision.

Other duties of managers

All duties other than the discharge of detained patients can be delegated to officers. These duties are:

- to accept a patient and record admission – form 14 (reg. 4(3))

- to give information to detained patients – section 132

- to give information to the nearest relative unless the patient requests otherwise – section 132(4)

- to give information to the nearest relative about the discharge of the patient unless the patient requests otherwise – section 133(1)

- to inform the nearest relative of the continued detention of the patient after a report from the responsible medical officer has been received – section 25(2)

- to discharge the patient if appropriate – section 23(2)(b) (cannot be delegated)

- to refer the patient to a mental health review tribunal – section 68(1)(2)

- to transfer a patient – section 19(3); section 19(1A); reg. 7(2) and reg. 7(3)

- to scrutinise and oversee the documentation and consider whether to give consent to rectification

- to oversee generally the care and treatment of the detained patient

- to monitor the handling of complaints.

Note, however, that the managers are still responsible for the overall care of all patients, detained and informal.

Not all these duties can be covered in detail in this session, but, by reference to the relevant sections of *Speller*, you can read up for yourself any area that is of interest to you.

5: Medical treatment for mental disorder

Read *Speller*, section 30.6, pp. 802-818, which covers the provision of Part IV of the Mental Health Act 1983 on consent to treatment.

Whilst these provisions might appear somewhat complex, they can be simplified as follows:

- Section 57 covers surgical operation for destroying brain tissue or for destroying the functioning of brain tissue and the implantation of hormones for reducing male sexual drive

- Section 58 covers electro-convulsive therapy and medication after three months or more have elapsed since medicine was first administered during that period of detention

- Section 63 covers all other treatments.

Section 57 requires the patient's consent and confirmation of his ability to consent by a registered medical practitioner and two other persons appointed by the Secretary of State (this power has been delegated to the Mental Health Act Commission); the registered medical practitioner must also certify that the treatment should be given. The two appointed people must consult two other persons who have been professionally concerned with the patient's medical treatment, one of whom must be a nurse and the other neither a nurse nor a registered medical practitioner.

Section 58 envisages two scenarios: one where the patient consents and the other where the patient refuses to consent or is unable to consent.

1 Where the patient is able and does consent.

In this situation the responsible medical officer or a registered medical practitioner appointed by the Secretary of State must certify in writing (on form 38) that the patient is capable of understanding the nature, purpose and likely effects of the treatment and has consented to it.

2 Where the patient refuses to consent or is unable to consent.

Here an independent registered medical practitioner, known as a second opinion appointed doctor (SOAD), must be brought in to examine the patient. If appropriate, he must then certify in writing (form 39) that the patient is not capable of understanding the nature, purpose and likely effects of that treatment or has not consented to it, but that, having regard to the likelihood of its alleviating or preventing a deterioration of his condition, the treatment should be given. The SOAD must consult with two persons professionally concerned with the patient's medical treatment, one of whom must be a nurse and the other neither a nurse nor a registered medical practitioner.

Section 63 treatment that does not come under sections 57 or 58 can be given without the patient's consent, provided it is for mental disorder and is given by, or under the direction of, the responsible medical officer.

Urgent treatments

In an emergency, treatment can be given under section 62, with the nature of the treatment depending on the degree of urgency. This also covers the situation where the patient has given agreement to a treatment plan under section 58, but then withdraws his consent and any of the situations envisaged in section 62 exists.

Treatment of detained patients for physical disorder

Part IV of the Mental Health Act only covers treatment for mental disorder. Detained patients who require treatment for physical conditions must give their consent unless they are deemed, as a result of their mental disorder, to lack the mental competence necessary to give a valid consent. In such circumstances they can be treated according to the decision in *Re F* (see the paragraph below).

Informal patients

Treatment cannot be given to informal patients without their consent unless there is a situation of necessity which justifies the use of common law powers. Refer back to section 5 of Session Four and the case of *Re F* in which the House of Lords stated that it was lawful for the professional to act out of necessity in the best interests of an incompetent patient by following the Bolam Test (*Speller*, pp. 263-264).

ACTIVITY 47   ALLOW **20** MINUTES

With reference to *Speller*, pp. 802-818, section 30.6, answer the following questions:

1 A patient is admitted under section 4, and her registered medical practitioner considers that she requires treatment. She is not prepared to give her consent. Can she be compelled to have it?

2 A patient detained under section 3 requires an appendectomy and refuses to give consent. Can he be compelled to have it?

3 A patient detained under section 3 is initially given no medication, but after two months the responsible medical officer decides that it is essential that he should receive medication. The patient refuses to give consent. At what point is it necessary for a second opinion appointed doctor to be brought in?

4 An elderly mentally infirm patient is admitted informally. She has refused to eat and is in an extremely depressed state. Her responsible medical practitioner considers that she needs to have electro-convulsive therapy. What is the legal position about administering this to her?

5 An informal patient becomes extremely disturbed and the nurses detain the patient under section 5(4). The responsible medical practitioner arrives within half an hour and considers that the patient should be given an injection immediately. What is the legal situation?

Commentary

1 No. Refer to *Speller*, pp. 803-804, from which you will see that Part IV of the Mental Health Act 1983 only affects certain detained patients. It does not apply to patients detained under sections 4, 5(4), 5(2), 35, 135, 136, 37(4) or a patient conditionally discharged under section 42(2), 73 or 74 who has not been recalled. This means that the patient must give consent for the treatment to be administered unless the situation set out in *Re F* exists.

2 Part IV of the Mental Health Act only refers to treatments for mental disorder, so the appendectomy cannot be covered under the provisions of the Act. Treatment can only be given without consent on the basis of *Re F*. A Broadmoor patient recently succeeded in obtaining an injunction preventing the hospital doctors amputating his foot without his consent. Refer back to the case in section 5 of Session Four: *Re C (Adult) (Refusal of Medical Treatment)* (1994).

3   The patient under section 3 will come under the provision of section 58 three months from the time at which he is first given medication. In this patient's case this will be five months after admission. Until that time medication can be given without his consent under section 63. However, after three months of medication he must either give a valid consent under section 58(3)(a) or be seen by a second opinion appointed doctor under section 58(3)(b).

4   Whilst technically the treatment could be given under the principles of *Re F*, in such circumstances it would be considered preferable for the patient to be detained under section 2, or 3 if she lacks the capacity to give consent, and for the initial treatment to be given under section 62 if a situation of urgency exists. The second opinion appointed doctor should be called in as soon as possible in order that the provision of section 58(3)(b) can be complied with.

5   Sections 5(4) and 5(2) are both excluded from Part IV of the Act. See the answer to question 1 above.

Summary

- The Mental Health Act 1983 gives provision for the admission and detention of mentally disordered people with safeguards against any abuse of this power.

- Guardianship is available for people who need close supervision but who do not need hospital treatment. The issue of care in the community is one that is currently being debated.

- Managers hearing an appeal for discharge should ensure that each party has the opportunity to present their case.

- Treatment can only be given for mental disorder either with the patient's consent or under certain conditions and safeguards, except when the circumstances of *Re F* prevail.

Before you move on to the final session, check that you have achieved the objectives given at the beginning of this session and, if not, review the appropriate section(s).

SESSION NINE

Specialist areas

Introduction

Not all of the topics covered in this session will relate to your area of work and it is therefore recommended that, rather than attempting to cover everything, you concentrate on those which are of greatest interest to you. However, whatever your choice, it is recommended that you undertake section 7, which looks at health care law in the future.

Session objectives

Depending upon your choice of sections, when you have completed this session, you should be able to:

- outline the specific laws and professional standards relating to the midwife and the supervisor of midwives

- explain the limitations on the use of organs from live and dead donors

- summarise the laws and regulations which relate to birth and death and to the termination of pregnancy

- describe the statutory framework set up in relation to medicines and the new laws relating to nurse prescribing

- discuss the legal regulation of human fertilisation, embryonic and genetic research

- summarise the rules relating to notifiable diseases and the regulations relating to HIV/AIDS.

1: Midwifery

Midwives are subject to all the laws relating to nurse practitioners, but in addition are subject to the *Midwives Rules* and to the specific provisions of the Medicines Act and other legislation relating to medicine which apply to the registered midwife. Alone of the registered practitioners at present, they have a statutory duty to attend refresher courses at least every five years, since without this they are unable to remain on the register. Whilst, like all practitioners registered by the UKCC they are subject to the *Code of Professional Conduct*, they are also subject to *A Midwife's Code of Practice*. From April 1995, all UKCC registered practitioners will have to comply with post-registration education requirements in order to remain on the register.

Read *Speller*, **section 19.6, pp. 541-548.**

ACTIVITY 48　　　　　ALLOW **15** MINUTES

Obtain a copy of the *Midwives Rules* (UKCC, 1991a) and *A Midwife's Code of Practice* (UKCC, 1991b). These should be available from your local school of midwifery or midwifery department; otherwise they can be obtained from the UKCC. Compare these documents with the *Code of Professional Conduct* (UKCC, 1992) for all registered practitioners with the UKCC.

The profession of midwifery is the only health profession which has a statutory duty to provide supervisors. Look at the provisions relating to the appointment and function of supervisors of midwifery and identify the advantages and disadvantages of a system of supervision. Note that the supervisor is not vicariously responsible for the work of the midwife whom she supervises; she is, however, personally liable for negligent advice and her own personal actions and omissions.

Commentary

As you will have seen, the registered midwife has a special place in law and the system of supervision is unique to midwifery. There are advantages in the supervision system both in the management field and also in the field of professional development. Supervisors of midwives are in a strong position to ensure that standards of midwifery practice are maintained by the health authorities and that individual midwives receive the necessary counselling and support to maintain their professional development.

2: Organ transplant and the use of the body after death

Transplants between live persons

The donation of organs from living donors was originally only subject to laws relating to consent and to the criminal laws of causing grievous bodily harm.

Following reports of a trade in organs from people living overseas, however, the Human Organ Transplants Act 1989 was passed which places restrictions and imposes criminal offences upon transplants between live persons. The Act does not apply to parts of the body which can be regenerated, such as blood and bone marrow.

> **Read *Speller*, section 25.2, pp. 663-668, noting the role of the Unrelated Live Transplant Regulation Authority (ULTRA) which is described in section 25.2.2.**

Transplants from dead bodies

> **Read *Speller*, section 25.1, pp. 653-663, and note the difference between the situations that come under section 1(1) and under section 1(2) of the Act.**

ACTIVITY 49   ALLOW 10 MINUTES

Imagine that you are the manager of a district general hospital when the following situations arise and in each case an organ transplant is considered. What would you advise?

1 A young man of 21 is brought into the accident and emergency department following a road accident. He is close to death and staff have found a donor card in his pocket. His parents are with him and say that they are not aware that he has ever changed his mind, but that they never agreed with his views and if asked for consent would refuse to give it.

2 Similar circumstances to those described above but the young man is not carrying a donor card. His mother says that she heard him state that he was personally in favour of organ donation, but the parents themselves have very different views and would never give their consent.

3 A girl of 10 falls from the roof of a shed. The staff know that her life cannot be saved. Her parents consent to her organs being used, but a distant aunt who is very attached to the girl and who comes to the intensive care unit says that she would disapprove of any donation of organs.

Commentary

Note that Section 1(1) of the Human Tissue Act does not require the consent of the relatives, merely a check to ensure that the dying person has not changed his mind since the card was completed. In case 1, therefore, the parents do not have to give their consent. However, it would be very unusual for a hospital to enforce the wishes of the dead person against the unwilling relatives, and therefore in such cases it is often the practice for the organs not to be taken. Note that since the death occurred in a road accident this would automatically be a coroner's case and there should be no touching of the body without notifying the coroner. In such cases the coroner is usually sympathetic to the use of the organs and could give his consent to the organs being taken.

In contrast, case 2 comes under Section 1(2) of the Act and, in the absence of two witnesses to the views of the deceased, the parents would have the right to object to the taking of organs.

Regarding case 3, under section 1(2) of the Act, the person in lawful possession of the body should check to see if the deceased or the spouse or any surviving relative objects to the body being so dealt with. This could therefore include the distant aunt who holds such strong views against organ donation. However, if the parents hold equally strong views and there was a tussle between parents and aunt, the person lawfully in possession of the body could probably authorise the organs to be taken on the basis of the consent of the parents. This type of situation has not been before the courts, so the law is not certain.

These cases highlight the problems relating to obtaining organs for transplant. Because of the demand for organs, it has been suggested that there should be a system of opting out rather than opting in: i.e. if a person has not declared himself to be hostile to the use of his organs, it should automatically be assumed that they are available for collection. Another suggestion is that there should be a statutory duty for staff in appropriate circumstances to ask relatives for consent to take the organs. This would possibly make it easier for staff to broach the subject. For instance: 'I am sorry to have to ask you this, but I am obliged by law to make this request. Would you agree to the use of your son's/daughter's/etc.'s organs for transplant?' It has been suggested that many more people would agree if a request were made.

Post-mortem examinations and use of the body for research and education

Speller, pp. 670–677, section 25.4, covers the carrying out of post-mortem examinations. If the body has been referred to the coroner and comes within his jurisdiction, then he has the right to request that a post mortem is carried out.

If medical staff are aware of the cause of death and are able to sign the death certificate but are interested to have more details about the deceased, then a post-mortem examination can only be carried out with the consent of the person lawfully in charge of the body, unless the provisions of section 1 of the Anatomy Act 1984 are satisfied.

3: Births and deaths in hospital and abortion

Read *Speller*, Chapter 24, pp. 647-651, which covers the duty to register births and deaths, noting the points made below.

1 Any live birth must be registered even if the baby dies shortly afterwards. It must be registered as a birth and as a death.

2 If a fetus of 24 weeks or more gestation is still born, then it must be registered as such.

3 If a fetus of less that 24 weeks' gestation is expelled from the womb without life, then it is not registerable either as a birth or a death and can be

disposed of in any manner which does not offend public decency.

A birth must be notified to the District Medical Officer and also registered. Note the penalties for failing to register. Note also the duties which fall upon the health professionals.

Abortion

> **Read *Speller*, Chapter 27, pp. 687-692, which covers the topic of the medical termination of pregnancy, known as abortion.**

The baby in the womb is not seen as having a legal personage. It can only bring an action if it survives. However, it is afforded some protection by the criminal laws, in particular the Infant Life (Preservation) Act 1929 and sections 58 and 59 of the Offences Against the Person Act 1861.

The Abortion Act 1967 must be seen against the background of this legislation and it gives protection from the force of those Acts providing its requirements are met. The age at which an abortion can lawfully be carried out has raised considerable concern, and the limit of 28 weeks originally set in the 1967 Act was replaced by 24 weeks under the amendments to the 1967 Act brought in by the Human Fertilisation and Embryology Act 1990. However, this does not mean that it is not lawful to carry out an abortion of a fetus of over 24 weeks' gestation, since, as can be seen from section 1(1) of the Act, set out in Speller, p. 686, the 24-week limit only applies to the circumstances described in paragraph (a) and does not apply to those in paragraphs (b), (c) or (d).

ACTIVITY 50	ALLOW 10 MINUTES

What would happen in the following circumstances?

1   A midwife is asked to assist in the gynaecology ward in carrying out prostaglandin terminations. She refuses on the ground that she trained to work as a midwife to deliver babies not to kill them.

2   A woman who has three children is 25 weeks' pregnant. She discovers that her husband has just been made redundant and she therefore wants an abortion on the grounds that they could not cope financially with an extra child.

3   Following amniocentesis, a woman discovers that her expected child is suffering from Down's syndrome and she considers abortion.

4   A girl of 15 years wishes to have an abortion and two doctors agree that the statutory requirements are satisfied. Her parents, however, argue that she is not capable of making up her own mind and they are prepared to look after the child as their own.

5   Following a lawful termination of pregnancy at 24 weeks, the aborted fetus is born alive.

Commentary

1 The midwife would be able to take advantage of the conscientious objection clause in the Act, providing that an emergency did not exist.

2 The woman would not be able to have an abortion unless she satisfied subsections 1(1) (b) or (c) or (d) of the amended Abortion Act 1967. She is precluded from relying upon (a) as the pregnancy is over 24 weeks. From the few facts given here it does not seem likely that any of the requirements would be satisfied.

3 Subsection 1(1)(d) enables an abortion to take place if two medical practitioners are satisfied that there is substantial risk that if the child were born it would suffer from such physical or mental abnormalities as to be seriously handicapped. There is no definition of this term, but Down's syndrome, especially if there were other congenital abnormalities, might well come within this subsection.

4 The parents of the pregnant girl have no legal right to give or withhold consent to the abortion if the child is herself capable of making a decision. If there are two medical practitioners who consider that the requirements of the Act are satisfied, the termination can proceed. You may remember the case of *Re P* we looked at in section 4 of Session Four.

5 If an aborted fetus is born alive, then every reasonable effort must be made to save it since the Act does not give power to kill a living child. Should it subsequently die, it should have both a birth certificate and a death certificate.

4: Medicines and poisons

Read *Speller*, Chapter 29, sections 29.1 to 29.4.2, pp. 697-719.

Notice the differences between the Medicines Act 1968 (*Speller*, section 29.1) – which provides the statutory framework for the manufacture, distribution, import, export, sale and supply of medicinal products and establishes a licensing system for the control of medicines – and the Misuse of Drugs Act 1971 (*Speller*, section 29.2) – which relates to controlled drugs. The latter Act also covers the control and treatment of drug addicts.

Classification of medicines

Under the Medicines Act 1968 there are the following categories:

General sales list
These are medicines which can be sold generally and a registered pharmacist is not required to be present at the sale. However, the size of the packs are restricted in such circumstances.

Sales only under the supervision of a registered pharmacist
Medicinal products which come under this category do not require a prescription but can only be sold in a retail pharmacy registered with the Royal Pharmaceutical Society.

Prescription-only medicines
Medicines in this category can only be given on a prescription by an appropriate practitioner. In 1992, specific nurse practitioners were added to the list of

authorised practitioners. However, the implementation of the legislation was delayed until 1994 and it will initially only apply in eight pilot areas in England.

Nurse prescribing

Statutory Instrument 1994 No. 2408 brought into effect Sections 1 and 2 of the Medicinal Products: Prescription by Nurses etc. Act 1992, on 3rd October 1994. Community nurses and health visitors who have undergone additional training are being allowed to prescribe in eight pilot areas from October 1994. The products they can prescribe are listed in a Nursing Formulary published by the British Medical Association and the Royal Pharmaceutical Society of Great Britain in conjunction with the Health Visitors' Association and the Royal College of Nursing. Following an evaluation of the pilot schemes, nurse prescribing is likely to be extended to other areas and to other categories of nurse practitioners.

Controlled drugs

The Misuse of Drugs Act 1971 has five schedules for categorising drugs. Details are given in *Speller*, section 29.2.

ACTIVITY 51   ALLOW **20** MINUTES

Track down a copy of the *British National Formulary* (BNF) for medicines which is published by the British Medical Association and the Royal Pharmaceutical Society of Great Britain and is updated every year. It should be easily available in a number of locations: your pharmacy, library, on wards or in individual departments. Read the introductory pages relating to the statutory regulations and advice for prescribing practitioners. Note in particular the format of the formulary and the identification of dosages, contraindications and the prices given. From 1995, the *Nurse Prescribers Formulary* will be bound in with the BNF. This has been prepared in conjunction with the Health Visitors' Association and the Royal College of Nursing.

Using the information you acquired when you studied the issue of consent to treatment in Session Four, consider the information which a registered practitioner should give to a patient when suggesting the prescription of a common drug such as aspirin, or any other drug you choose.

Ask the pharmacist if you can see an example of a leaflet for any drug which the manufacturers send with the product.

Commentary

The BNF is up-dated every year and is the standard reference work for those who prescribe, dispense and administer drugs. It also gives the prices of drugs so that the practitioner has an understanding of the costs of the medicines prescribed. Concern has been expressed in recent years that patients should receive more information relating to the side effects of medicines so that the consent they give to taking the recommended medication is informed. There are specialist publications which give the general public more information on the purpose and likely effects of the drugs. Refer back to section 1 of Session Four and note that, in the Sidaway case, the House of Lords stated that the doctrine of informed consent was not recognised in this country.

Crown immunity

You may recall from earlier in this unit that the protection which health authorities have enjoyed in their capacity as crown authorities has been gradually eroded. First this was by the National Health Service (Amendment) Act 1986, which removed the immunity in relation to health and safety legislation and food legislation. Further removals took place under the NHS and Community Care Act 1990, which left only a few areas of immunity (see section 4 of Session Three). One of the areas affected by the 1990 Act is that of the law relating to medicines and drugs. Speller, section 29.4, sets out the effect of the removal of crown status in this field. At the time of writing the situation was still unclear.

5: Human fertilisation, embryo research and genetic discoveries

We noted earlier in this session how the Human Fertilisation and Embryology Act 1990 amended the provisions of the Abortion Act 1967. These changes were, however, incidental to the main purpose of this legislation which was:

'1 to make provision in connection with human embryos and any subsequent development of such embryos;

2 to prohibit certain practices in connection with embryos and gametes;

3 to establish a Human Fertilisation and Embryology Authority;

4 to make provision about the persons who in certain circumstances are to be treated in law as the parents of the child;

5 and to amend the Surrogacy Arrangements Act 1985.'

Human Fertilisation and Embryology Act 1990

The Act in the main incorporates the recommendations of the majority of the Warnock Committee (1984) who reported on the extent to which experimentation on human embryos should be allowed and the laws relating to the placing of embryos into humans. The Authority has now been established and it regulates through a licensing mechanism the functions of those organisations which arrange for embryos to be grown and implanted. You are strongly urged to study the annual report of the Authority since this gives a good perspective of its functions and this topic is not covered in *Speller*.

The Act does not deal with the legal implications of genetic discoveries. These have been the subject of the Clothier Committee which presented the report, *The Ethics of Gene Therapy*, to Parliament in January 1992. Amongst its recommendations it suggested that:

1 Somatic gene therapy (i.e. gene therapy which only affects the individual and not future generations) should be conducted according to the principles which guide research involving human subjects.

2 Gene line therapy should not yet be attempted.

3 A supervisory body should be established to be responsible for developing a protocol for conducting research and treatment.

4 Local research ethics committees should be an effective means of control and discipline over the conduct of gene therapy.

At present there are no laws regulating the handling of genetic information other than the advisory bodies set up as described above. The development of techniques in genetic diagnosis are improving and, as progress is made in diagnosing particular genetic predispositions, there will be concern about protecting at-risk individuals from pressure by insurance companies and employers to undergo genetic testing which could affect an individual's ability to obtain life insurance cover or employment.

The National Council of Bioethics was established in 1991 to consider the ethical issues presented by advances in bio-medical and biological research. Genetic screening was the subject of its first report (National Council of Bioethics, 1993), which emphasised the need for adequately informed consent and the need for the Department of Health to keep under review genetic screening by employers and insurance companies.

ACTIVITY 52 — ALLOW 10 MINUTES

1 List the arguments for permitting insurance companies to have a right to insist that an individual undergoes genetic testing and that the results are passed on to the insurance company.

2 List the arguments in favour of protecting the individual against such compulsory testing.

Commentary

Similar arguments to those raised about this issue have emerged in relation to the insistence by insurance companies on knowing whether an applicant has been tested for HIV infection. Insurance cover is based on the principle of *uberrimae fidei*, i.e. maximum trust. The applicant must disclose any information which may affect the insurance terms. If he fails to do so, the insurance contract can be set aside. The insurance company is entitled to know the nature of the risk for which it is providing cover. On the other hand, an individual would be gravely prejudiced, particularly as the genetic testing might only reveal a possibility, not the certainty, that a disease would later develop. A compromise was developed with HIV/AIDS infections in that the insurance companies did not insist upon a medical test for HIV/AIDS, but omitted cover for that contingency from the policy. This is not, however, a realistic solution for genetic testing for a wide variety of disorders. If it is felt that insurance companies have the right to all relevant information, the state would presumably have to accept a duty to those of its citizens who cannot protect themselves against future misfortune through insurance cover, or obtain a mortgage.

6: The notification of infectious diseases and HIV/AIDS infections

Speller, chapter 28, explains the definition of diseases that are notifiable and the procedure which must be followed when a notifiable disease or a case of food poisoning is diagnosed. The duty to notify is placed upon the registered medical practitioner who becomes aware that a patient is suffering from a notifiable disease. There are rules relating to the disposal of dead bodies to prevent infection and the powers of compulsory removal to hospital of a person suffering from a notifiable disease.

AIDS infections were made notifiable under regulation 3 of the Public Health (Infectious Diseases) Regulations 1988, but come under separate regulations in relation to the collection of information and the right to be transferred to a place of safety; see *Speller*, pp. 694-695.

Read *Speller*, Chapter 28, pp. 693-696.

ACTIVITY 53   ALLOW 20 MINUTES

1 Explain to one of your colleagues, as if to a newly qualified general practitioner, the law relating to the notification of infectious diseases.

2 The duty to inform the specified authority of the existence of a notifiable disease and the right compulsorily to remove a sufferer to a hospital are examples where the individual rights of the patient are sacrificed to the public interest. With reference to the discussion on confidentiality in Session Five, list what criteria you think should exist before individual rights are overruled.

3 A general practitioner is informed that one of his patients is HIV positive. The wife of this patient is also on the GP's list. Do you consider that the GP has a duty to inform the wife? Does your answer depend upon the fact that the wife is also his patient?

Commentary

Your answer to question 1 should cover the main points in *Speller*, section 28.2.

The Government has opted to legislate for AIDS statistics to be collected separately from the Public Health (Control of Disease) Act 1984 and passed the AIDS (Control) Act 1987. In addition, under the Public Health Act (Infectious Disease) Regulations 1985, powers are given to the local authorities to apply to a Justice of the Peace for the removal of an AIDS sufferer to hospital to be detained there, or to arrange for the medical examination of a person believed to be suffering from AIDS. These powers came into force on 22 March 1985.

Balancing the rights of the individual against the duty to the public is recognised as a necessity by most professional bodies. An example of one set of criteria is that given by the UKCC in its advisory paper on confidentiality (UKCC, 1987).

For question 3, disclosure to the wife could be justified on the grounds that it is in the public interest to protect the wife from the possibility of being infected with AIDS. The best course would be for the doctor to advise the patient that he should inform his wife of the risk of infection, and that if the patient fails to do so, then the doctor would consider that it was his duty to inform the wife of the risk to her health. There is no decided case on the question.

7: Health care law in the future

So far in this session we have looked at only a few of the specialist areas of law which exist within health care. You may have other professional concerns that you can follow up in *Speller*. You should also aim to keep informed about changes in the law relating to health care. There are frequently cases which relate to the health services, particularly in the field of negligence and claims for compensation. Be alert to the reports of these cases in the media and changes in the statutes relating to health care.

ACTIVITY 54   ONGOING

Using reputable newspapers, journals and other sources, start a collection of cuttings of news items relating to health care litigation, criminal charges and professional disciplinary hearings of health professionals, and to any proposed changes in the law relating to health care provision. Refer to this unit and to *Speller* to examine the implications of any news items you come across.

Commentary

This activity should show you how frequently the health services and their staff feature in the news and the implications for the law. This should become a regular activity and you should find that the work undertaken in this unit provides a useful foundation on which you can build your knowledge and understanding. Proposed changes in the law relating to health care should acquire a new significance for you and you should be able to enter the debate with informed understanding of the implications of any proposed changes.

Summary

- Midwives are subject to specific legal and professional standards.

- There are legal restrictions on the transplant of organs and the use of a body for research and education.

- There are laws governing the registration of birth and death and the circumstances under which abortion is permitted.

- The manufacture, distribution and supply of medicines and drugs are controlled by a number of statutes.

- The main recommendations of the Warnock Committee (1984) have been incorporated into the Human Fertilisation and Embryology Act 1990. Genetic discoveries were the subject of the Clothier Committee report (1992).

- There are procedures to be followed in the event of certain diseases being diagnosed, as well as in the event of food poisoning or HIV/AIDS infections.

Now that you have completed this session, check that you have achieved the relevant objectives given at the beginning and, if not, review the appropriate section(s). You can then go on to complete the Learning Review that follows this session.

LEARNING REVIEW

Now that you have completed your work on this unit, you may like to assess your progress and understanding. You can do this by completing the following learning review and comparing your answers with those that you gave before you started Session One.

	Not at all	Partly	Quite well	Very well

Session One

I can:

- explain the basic technical legal terms and the framework of the civil and criminal legal system ☐ ☐ ☐ ☐
- describe the basic principles of accountability ☐ ☐ ☐ ☐
- discuss the relationship between codes of professional conduct and legal duties and powers ☐ ☐ ☐ ☐
- specify the circumstances which can lead to legal action being taken ☐ ☐ ☐ ☐
- minimise the risk of litigation through sound practices ☐ ☐ ☐ ☐
- summarise the defences which may be available. ☐ ☐ ☐ ☐

Session Two

I can:

- define a contract of employment ☐ ☐ ☐ ☐
- summarise the legal rights of employers and employees ☐ ☐ ☐ ☐
- discuss the implementation of employment policies at my workplace ☐ ☐ ☐ ☐
- describe procedures for redundancy and the legal rights of trade unions. ☐ ☐ ☐ ☐

Session Three

I can:

- summarise the main provisions of the Health and Safety at Work Act 1974 regarding the appointment and duties of safety representatives ☐ ☐ ☐ ☐

	Not at all	Partly	Quite well	Very well

Session Three *continued*

- discuss specific health and safety regulations applicable in my workplace ☐ ☐ ☐ ☐

- apply the health and safety regulations to my workplace and take preventative measures in relation to health and safety ☐ ☐ ☐ ☐

- specify the key stages in the assessment of risk ☐ ☐ ☐ ☐

- discuss measures to promote the creation and maintenance of a health and safety culture ☐ ☐ ☐ ☐

- discuss the enforcement provisions for health and safety in the health services ☐ ☐ ☐ ☐

- relate health and safety to professional and contractual responsibilities ☐ ☐ ☐ ☐

- give illustrations of legal liability for health and safety. ☐ ☐ ☐ ☐

Session Four

I can:

- discuss the duty to inform the patient, supported by the authority of legal cases ☐ ☐ ☐ ☐

- describe the different methods of gaining consent and what constitutes consent ☐ ☐ ☐ ☐

- explain the circumstances when treatment can be given without the patient's consent ☐ ☐ ☐ ☐

- give an account of the legal principles regarding consent to treatment which apply to specific categories such as children and mentally disordered people ☐ ☐ ☐ ☐

- highlight the problems inherent in advance directives and suggest solutions ☐ ☐ ☐ ☐

- discuss the withdrawal of treatment in the best interest of the patient ☐ ☐ ☐ ☐

- explain the principles and procedures regarding the use of patients for teaching and research. ☐ ☐ ☐ ☐

Session Five

I can:

- debate the issue of 'whistle-blowing' in the light of the NHS Management Executive's guidelines ☐ ☐ ☐ ☐

	Not at all	Partly	Quite well	Very well

Session Five *continued*

- discuss the duty of confidentiality and summarise the circumstances in which it does not apply ☐ ☐ ☐ ☐
- describe the main provisions of the Data Protection Act 1984 ☐ ☐ ☐ ☐
- explain the statutory rights of access to health records held in manual form and to medical reports prepared for employment or insurance purposes ☐ ☐ ☐ ☐
- specify the legal requirements relating to the ownership and preservation of records. ☐ ☐ ☐ ☐

Session Six

I can:

- describe how the internal market works and debate the provision of health care ☐ ☐ ☐ ☐
- discuss the administrative structure of the health service and the function of the statutory authorities ☐ ☐ ☐ ☐
- summarise the advisory and consultative machinery which supports a dialogue between professionals and the authorities, and across different kinds of authority ☐ ☐ ☐ ☐
- give an account of the role of community health councils ☐ ☐ ☐ ☐
- outline the mechanism to regulate the relationship between purchasers and providers ☐ ☐ ☐ ☐
- discuss the procedures for the handling of complaints ☐ ☐ ☐ ☐
- define the role of the Health Service Commissioner and the Mental Health Act Commission. ☐ ☐ ☐ ☐

Session Seven

I can:

- discuss liability for the property of staff, patients and their visitors ☐ ☐ ☐ ☐
- specify the procedure that should be adopted when a patient wishes to draw up a will ☐ ☐ ☐ ☐
- explain the restrictions on search and arrest by employers or managers. ☐ ☐ ☐ ☐

	Not at all	Partly	Quite well	Very well

Session Eight

I can:

- explain the law regarding the detention and treatment of mentally disordered patients

| | ☐ | ☐ | ☐ | ☐ |

- describe the regulation of leave of absence under the Mental Health Act 1983

| | ☐ | ☐ | ☐ | ☐ |

- discuss the issues of guardianship and care in the community

| | ☐ | ☐ | ☐ | ☐ |

- detail the duties of managers including that of hearing appeals for discharge

| | ☐ | ☐ | ☐ | ☐ |

- explain the circumstances in which treatment can and cannot be given under the Mental Health Act 1983.

| | ☐ | ☐ | ☐ | ☐ |

Session Nine

I can:

- discuss the legal and professional responsibilities that are specific to midwives

| | ☐ | ☐ | ☐ | ☐ |

- describe the legal position with regard to organ transplant and the use of the body after death

| | ☐ | ☐ | ☐ | ☐ |

- identify the legal position regarding abortion and the registration of births and deaths

| | ☐ | ☐ | ☐ | ☐ |

- explain the legislation in the area of medicines and poisons

| | ☐ | ☐ | ☐ | ☐ |

- summarise the aims of the Human Fertilisation and Embryology Act 1990 and discuss issues raised by developments in genetic research

| | ☐ | ☐ | ☐ | ☐ |

- describe the procedures to be followed when a notifiable disease or case of food poisoning is diagnosed.

| | ☐ | ☐ | ☐ | ☐ |

RESOURCES SECTION

Contents

RESOURCE I

Law Report, The Times, July, 1994.

Proving involuntary manslaughter

Regina v Adomako

Before Lord Mackay of Clashfern, Lord Chancellor, Lord Keith of Kinkel, Lord Goff of Chieveley, Lord Browne-Wilkinson and Lord Woolf

[Speeches June 30]

The ingredients to be proved to establish an offence of involuntary manslaughter by breach of duty were the existence of the duty, breach of that duty which caused death and gross negligence which the jury considered justified a criminal conviction.

The House of Lords so held in dismissing an appeal brought by John Asare Adomako against the dismissal by the Court of Appeal (*sub nom*: *R v Prentice* (*The Times* May 21, 1993; [1994] QB 302)) of his appeal against conviction for manslaughter.

Lord Williams of Mostyn, QC and Mr James Watson for the appellant; Miss Ann Curnow, QC and Mr Anthony Leonard for the Crown.

THE LORD CHANCELLOR said that the conviction arose out of the conduct of an operation at the Mayday Hospital, Croydon on January 4, 1987. The appellant was, during the latter part of the operation, the anaesthetist in charge of the patient.

At approximately 11.05 am a disconnection occurred at the endotracheal tube connection. The supply of oxygen to the patient ceased and led to a cardiac arrest at 11.14 am. During that period the appellant failed to notice or remedy the disconnection.

The appellant first became aware that something was amiss when an alarm sounded on the Dinamap machine, which monitored the patient's blood pressure. From the evidence it appeared that some four and a half minutes would have elapsed between the disconnection and the sounding of the alarm.

When the alarm sounded the appellant responded in various ways by checking the equipment and by administering atropine to raise the patient's pulse. But at no stage before the cardiac arrest did he check the integrity of the endotracheal tube connection. The disconnection itself was not discovered until after resuscitation measures had been commenced.

It was conceded on behalf of the appellant at trial that he had been negligent. The issue was whether his conduct was criminal.

The Court of Appeal had held that except in cases of motor manslaughter, the ingredients which had to be proved to establish an offence of involuntary manslaughter by breach of duty were the existence of the duty, a breach of the duty which had caused death and gross negligence which the jury considered sufficient to justify a criminal conviction.

The jury might properly find gross negligence on proof of indifference to an obvious risk of injury to health or of actual foresight of the risk coupled either with a determination nevertheless to run it or with an intention to avoid it but involving such a high degree of negligence in the attempted avoidance as the jury considered justified conviction or of inattention or failure to advert to a serious risk going beyond mere inadvertence in respect of an obvious and important matter which the defendant's duty demanded he should address.

The reason the Court of Appeal excepted the cases of motor manslaughter and their formulation of the law was the decision of the House of Lords in *R v Seymour* (*Edward*) ([1983] 2 AC 493) in which it was held that where manslaughter was charged and the circumstances were that the victim was killed as a result of the reckless driving of the defendant on a public highway, the trial judge should give the jury the direction which had been suggested in *R v Lawrence* (*Stephen*) ([1982] AC 510) but that it was appropriate also to point out that in order to constitute the offence of manslaughter the risk of death being caused by the manner of the defendant's driving must be very high.

In his Lordship's opinion, the law as stated in *R v Bateman* ([1925] 19 Cr App R 8) and *Andrews v DPP* ([1937] AC 576) was satisfactory as providing a proper basis for describing the crime of involuntary manslaughter. Since the decision in *Andrews* was a House of Lords decision, it remained the most authoritative statement of the present law.

On that basis, the ordinary principles of the law of negligence applied to ascertain whether or not the defendant had been in breach of a duty of care towards the victim who had died.

If such a breach of duty was established the next question was whether that breach of duty caused the death of the victim.

If so, the jury had to go on to consider whether that breach of duty should be characterised as gross negligence and therefore as a crime. That would depend on the seriousness of the breach of duty committed by the defendant in all the circumstances in which the defendant was placed when it occurred.

The jury would have to consider whether the extent to which the defendant's conduct departed from the proper standard of care incumbent upon him, involving as it must have done a risk of death to the patient, was such that it should be judged criminal.

However, the law as stated in *Seymour* should no longer apply since the underlying statutory provisions on which it rested had now been repealed by the Road Traffic Act 1991.

It might be that cases of involuntary motor manslaughter would as a result become rare but his Lordship considered it satisfactory that there should be any exception to the generality of the statement which his Lordship had made.

It was perfectly appropriate that the word "reckless" should be used in cases of involuntary manslaughter.

It was quite unnecessary in the context of gross negligence to give the detailed directions with regard to the meaning of the word "reckless" associated with *Lawrence*.

Accordingly, the appeal would be dismissed and the certified question should be answered by saying that in cases of manslaughter by criminal negligence involving a breach of duty, it was a sufficient direction to the jury to adopt the gross negligence test set out by the Court of Appeal in the present case following *Bateman* and *Andrews* and that it was not necessary to refer to the definition of recklessness in *Lawrence*, although it was perfectly open to the trial judge to use the word "reckless" in its ordinary meaning as part of his exposition of the law if he deemed it appropriate in the circumstances of the particular case.

Lord Keith, Lord Goff, Lord Browne-Wilkinson and Lord Woolf agreed.

Solicitors: Bindman & Partners; Crown Prosecution Services Headquarters

Cost of spillage from cup of tea

RESOURCE 2

The Times, June 13, 1989.

Bell v Department of Health and Social Security

Before Mr Justice Drake
[Judgment June 12]

Where there was a history of spillage of liquids on pseudo-marble passages in a departmental office-block, the department's obligations to their employees at common law and by statute would not be discharged simply by entreating the employees to take more care when carrying such things as tea or coffee over them.

Mr Justice Drake so held in the Queen's Bench Division in entering judgment for the plaintiff, Joan Bell, against the Department of Health and Social Security in the sum of £7,000 in general damages and £275 special damages, with interest, in respect of their negligence and breaches of statutory duty under section 2 of the Occupiers' Liability Act 1957 and under section 16 of the Offices, Shops and Railways Premises Act 1963.

Section 2 of the 1957 Act provides: "(1) An occupier of premises owes the same duty, the 'common duty of care', to all his visitors...

"(2) The common duty of care is a duty to take such care as in all the circumstances of the case is reasonable to see that the visitor will be reasonably safe in using the premises for the purposes for which he is invited or permitted by the occupier to be there."

Section 16 of the Offices, Shops and Railway Premises Act 1963 provides: "(1) All floors ... [and] passages ... comprised in premises to which this Act applies shall be ... properly maintained and shall, so far as is reasonably practicable, be kept free ... from any substance likely to cause persons to slip."

Mr Jeremy McMullen for the plaintiff; Mr Robert Jay for the defendant.

MR JUSTICE DRAKE said that the plaintiff was a married lady, aged 56, who had since 1974 been employed by the defendant department in a four-storey office block.

The department did not provide tea or coffee or utensils for their employees there; but they did provide employees with hot water to make their own drinks from a kitchen on the fourth floor.

There were two lifts: a small, automatic one, with a door operated by a push-button, and a larger lift whose doors had to be pulled to and fro by hand.

Some employees used to travel to the kitchen to fetch water which they then carried back to their offices; others carried mugs or cups to the kitchen and having infused their tea or coffee there carried them back, using one or other of the lifts.

On the afternoon of July 30, 1984 the plaintiff, whose office was on the third floor, was passing by the larger of the two lifts when she slipped on a small amount of liquid which, on the balance of probabilities, had been spilt onto the pseudo-marble surface of the passage by someone emerging from that lift while carrying a receptacle containing tea or coffee or hot water. In falling, she had hurt her hand, her chest and her coccyx.

The first question was whether the department's system for checking and dealing with such spillages as occurred had been adequate. On that, *Ward v Tesco Stores Ltd* ([1976] 1 WLR 810), had been cited: but the situation in a supermarket was very different from that in an office, and on the evidence his Lordship was satisfied that in providing for regular inspections of the building by a competent safety officer, a reasonable system had been established.

The second question was whether the department had done all they reasonably could have to prevent spillages occurring and on the principle in *Edwards v National Coal Board* ([1949] 1 KB 704) the likelihood of spillages occurring had to be weighed against the cost of the measures necessary to eliminate that risk.

The records had shown that spillages in that block had been common, so that it had been almost inevitable that sooner or later an accident would occur: indeed staff had several times each year, by means of bulletins, been besought to take better care and to put a a saucer or tray beneath any cup or mug which they carried from the kitchen.

The first measure, suggested on behalf of the plaintiff, had been the provision of a distribution point for hot water on each of the lower three floors of the building - thus minimising the distance employees would have to travel and obviating any need to use a lift.

His Lordship had not been told what that would have cost, but apparently it had been planned even before the accident and such further points had been installed in 1985.

Next, it was suggested that the department could have supplied appropriate saucers, cups and trays: their answer, that they had not the funds to buy such, his Lordship had not found acceptable.

Third, the risk of slipping could have been eliminated by providing some suitable non-slip surface over the pseudo-marble.

His Lordship had found this a borderline case: but after some hesitation (and indeed a change of mind) he had come to the conclusion that the department could and should have adopted measures to lessen the obvious risks their employees were running in all three of the respects mentioned. There would accordingly be judgment for the plaintiff.

Solicitors: Pattinson & Brewer; Treasury Solicitor

RESOURCE 3

Section 2, 1974.

Health and Safety at Work Act

General Duties of employers to their employees

(1) It shall be the duty of every employer to ensure, so far as is reasonably practicable, the health, safety and welfare at work of all his employees.

(2) Without prejudice to the generality of an employer's duty under the preceding subsection, the matters to which that duty extends include in particular:

(a) The provision and maintenance of plant and systems of work that are, so far as is reasonably practicable, safe and without risks to health;

(b) arrangements for ensuring, so far as is reasonably practicable, safety and absence of risks to health in connection with the use, handling, storage and transport of articles and substances;

(c) the provision of such information, instruction, training and supervision as is necessary to ensure, so far as is reasonably practicable, the health and safety at work of his employees;

(d) so far as is reasonably practicable as regards any place of work under the employer's control, the maintenance of it in a condition that is safe and without risks to health and the provision and maintenance of means of access to and egress from it that are safe and without such risks;

(e) the provision and maintenance of a working environment for his employees that is, so far as is reasonably practicable, safe, without risks to health and adequate as regards facilities and arrangements for their welfare at work.

(3) Except in such cases as may be prescribed, it shall be the duty of every employer to prepare and as often as may be appropriate revise a written statement of his general policy with respect to the health and safety at work of his employees and the organisation and arrangements for the time being in force for carrying out that policy, and to bring the statement and any revision of it to the notice of all of his employees.

(4) Regulations made by the Secretary of State may provide for the appointment in prescribed cases by recognised trade unions (within the meaning of the regu-

lations) of safety representatives from amongst the employees, and those representatives shall represent the employees in consultations with the employers under the subsection (6) below and shall have other functions as may be prescribed.

(5)(Repealed).

(6)It shall be the duty of every employer to consult any such representatives with a view to the making and maintenance of arrangements which will enable him and his employees to co-operate effectively in promoting and developing measures to ensure the health and safety at work of the employees, and in checking the effectiveness of such measures.

(7)In such cases as may be prescribed it shall be the duty of every employer, if requested to do so by the safety representatives mentioned in subsections (4) and (5) above, to establish, in accordance with regulations made by the Secretary of State, a safety committee having the function of keeping under review the measures taken to ensure the health and safety at work of his employees and such other functions as may be prescribed.

Health and Safety at Work Act

RESOURCE 4

Section 20, 1974.

(2)The powers of an inspector referred to in the preceding subsection are the following, namely:

(a) at any reasonable time (or, in a situation which in his opinion is or may be dangerous, at any time) to enter any premises which he has reason to believe it is necessary for him to enter for the purpose mentioned in subsection (1) above;

(b) to take with him a constable if he has reasonable cause to apprehend any serious obstruction in the execution of his duty;

(c) without prejudice to the preceding paragraph, on entering any premises by virtue of paragraph (a) above to take with him:

  (i) any other person duly authorised by his (the inspector's) enforcing authority; and

  (ii)any equipment or materials required for any purpose for which the power of entry is being exercised;

(d) to make such examination and investigation as may in any circumstances be necessary for the purpose mentioned in subsection (1) above;

(e) as regards any premises which he has power to enter to direct that those premises or any part of them, or anything therein, shall be left undisturbed, (whether generally or in particular respects) for so long as is reasonably necessary for the purpose of any examination or investigation under paragraph (d) above;

(f) to take such measurements and photographs and make such records as he considers necessary for the purpose of any examination or investigation under paragraph (d) above;

(g) to take samples of any articles or substances found in any premises which he has power to enter, and of the atmosphere in or in the vicinity of any such premises;

(h)in the case of any article or substance found in any premises which he has power to enter, being an article or substance which appears to him to have caused or to be likely to cause danger to health or safety, to cause it to be dismantled or subjected to any process or test (but not so as to damage or destroy it unless this is in the circumstances necessary for the purpose mentioned in subsection (1) above).

(i) in the case of any such article or substance as is mentioned in the preceding paragraph, to take possession of it and detain it for so long as is necessary for all or any of the following purposes, namely:

  (i) to examine it and do to it anything which he has power to do under that paragraph;

  (ii) to ensure that it is not tampered with before his examination of it is completed;

  (iii) to ensure that it is available for use as evidence in any proceedings for an offence under any of the relevant statutory provisions or any proceedings relating to a notice under section 21 or 22;

(j) if he is conducting an examination or investigation under (d) to require any person ... to answer any questions as the inspector thinks fit and to sign a declaration of the truth of his answers ...

(k)to require production of, inspect and

take copies of any entry in any books or documents ...

(l) to require any person to afford himself such facilities and assistance within that person's control or responsibilities

as are necessary for him to exercise his powers;

(m)any other power which is necessary for the purpose of exercising any of the above powers.

RESOURCE 5

NHS Management Executive, 1993.

Guidance for staff on relations with the public and the media

Introduction

1 This guidance sets out the rights and responsibilities of staff when raising issues of concern about health care matters. The guidance does not affect existing guidance on statutory complaints procedures (as set out in HC(88)37), and it does not change or replace any nationally agreed terms and conditions of employment which give particular groups of employees freedom to speak and write.

2 The guidance complements professional or ethical rules, guidelines and codes of conduct on freedom of speech, such as, for example the UKCC Code of Professional Conduct, A Midwife's Code of Practice, and the GMC Guidance on Contractual Arrangements in Health Care. It is not intended to restrict the publication of clinical or scientific research findings or Annual Reports from Directors of Public Health.

Purpose of guidance

3 This guidance aims to make plain that:

(i) Individual members of staff in the NHS have a right and a duty to raise with their employers any matters of concern they may have about health service issues concerned with the delivery of care or services to a patient or client in their authority, Trust or unit.

(ii) Every NHS manager has a duty to ensure that staff are easily able to express their concerns through all levels of management to the employing authority or Trust. Managers must ensure that any staff concerns are dealt with thoroughly and fairly.

(iii)NHS employers should ensure that local policies and procedures are introduced to allow these rights and duties to be fully and properly met.

(iv)Individual members of staff in the NHS have an obligation to safeguard all confidential information to which they have access: particularly information about individual patients or clients, which is under all circumstances strictly confidential.

Key principles - putting patients first

4 The NHS exists to meet the needs of patients. The key principle of this guidance is that their individual interests must be paramount. Of course consultants have ultimate responsibility for the care of patients, but all NHS employees have a duty to draw to the attention of their managers any matter they consider to be damaging to the interests of a patient or client and to put forward suggestions which may improve their care. In the case of a patient or a client detained under the Mental Health Act, staff can also raise concerns with the Mental Health Act Commission.

5 So the normal working culture of the NHS should foster openness. Staff should be encouraged freely to contribute their views on all aspects of health service activities, especially about delivery of care and services to patients or clients. Free expression of these views can contribute to improving services for patients or clients in the future. NHS Managers are therefore expected to ensure that all staff are given every opportunity to make their contribution. Moreover, they must feel that their legitimate views will be welcomed, appreciated and, where appropriate, acted on positively.

6 **Under no circumstances are employees who express their views about health service issues in accordance with this guidance to be penalised in any way for doing so.**

7 An important principle of this guidance is that it should be for local management in consultation with all staff and local staff representatives to implement it in a way that is appropriate to local circumstances. They will wish to consider how best to promote a culture of openness and dialogue which at the same time upholds

patient confidentiality, does not unreasonably undermine confidence in the service and meets the obligations of staff to their employer.

Confidentiality to patients and employers – the responsibilities of staff

8   All NHS staff have a duty of confidentiality to patients. Unauthorised disclosure of personal information about any patient or client will be regarded as a most serious matter which will always warrant disciplinary action. This applies even where a member of staff believes that he or she is acting in the best interests of a patient or client by disclosing personal information.

9   Employees also have an implied duty of confidentiality and loyalty to their employer. Breach of this duty may result in disciplinary action, whether or not there is a clause in their contract of employment expressly addressing the question of confidentiality.

10 The duty of confidence to an employer is not absolute, however. In any case involving disclosure of confidential information, it may be claimed that the disclosure was made in the public interest. Such a justification might, in a disputed case, need to be defended and so should be soundly based. As a matter of prudence then, any employee who is considering making a disclosure of confidential information because they consider it to be in the public interest, should first seek specialist advice. This could be, for example, from one of the representative or regulatory organisations mentioned in paragraph 23 et seq.

11 Any explicit confidentiality provision in an individual staff employment contract must be expressed in a way that does not conflict in any way with the principles and advice set out in this guidance.

Establishing local procedures for dealing with staff concerns

12 All NHS employers should establish procedures locally - after full consultation with staff and local staff representatives - for handling staff concerns about health care issues, other than those to which the statutory complaints procedures apply, or which fall to established grievance procedures.

13 The local procedures may address in more detail any aspect of this guidance, provided that, in doing so, they do not conflict with the principles and advice set out in it. The procedures should allow for staff concerns to be considered at the highest levels of local management, including the General Manager or Chief Executive of the employing authority or

Trust. Procedures should include clear time limits for dealing with staff concerns.

Informal procedures

14 Of course, the aim should always be for staff concerns about health service issues to be resolved informally - between the individual and his or her line or professional managers. Managers should always:
- take concerns seriously; and
- consider them fully and sympathetically; and
- recognise that raising a concern can be a difficult experience for some staff; and
- seek advice from health care professionals where appropriate.

15 Staff who are not in a formal line management relationship (eg consultants) should discuss their concerns with relevant colleagues and then, if necessary, take them up directly with the General Manager or Chief Executive.

16 Where a staff concern can be acted upon, action should be taken promptly and the member of staff notified quickly of the action taken. Where action is not considered practicable or appropriate, the individual member of staff should be given a prompt and thorough explanation of the reasons for this. They should also be told what further action is available under local procedures.

Formal procedures

17 Where this informal approach proves ineffective, local procedures should provide for the matter to be referred up formally through the employee's management line. Where there are a number of management levels, each level of management should give the same thorough and fair consideration to the issue and advise the member of staff promptly of the outcome, within an agreed timetable. Again, the arrangements will need to be slighly different for staff not in a direct line management relationship - see paragraph 15 above.

18 Local procedures should make plain whether the employee may be accompanied or represented by his or her professional organisation or trade union representative, or other person of his or her choice, during this process.

19 The formal procedures should always provide for the employee to raise his or her concern, where necessary, with the highest level of local management. If an issue remains unresolved after it has been referred to all levels of management, the local formal procedures should provide for the individual member of staff to raise

his or her concern finally with the Chairman of the authority or Trust.

20 The Chairman may choose to deal with the matter personally or, for example where the concern is about action taken or decisions made by individual senior managers, in conjunction with non-executive board members. The Chairman may also choose to consult other suitable persons or bodies about the staff concern. Any action taken by the Chairman will need to be within the agreed timetable (see paragraph 17).

The designated officer

21 The procedural model set out above could prove unnecessarily cumbersome and time-consuming when dealing with concerns expressed by staff in extended management chains. As an alternative to using all the levels of the management chain, employers might prefer, in consultation with staff and local staff representatives, to designate a senior officer to whom matters unresolved by immediate line managers could be referred directly by the member of staff concerned. This could, though need not, be the officer designated to receive formal complaints under statutory procedures.

22 In a case where this procedure has been followed and the individual member of staff remains dissatisfied, the matter will need to be referred to the Chairman of the authority or Trust for action.

Reference to other bodies
Representative and regulatory organisations

23 All staff must retain the right to consult, seek guidance and support from their professional organisation or trade union, and from statutory bodies such as the United Kingdom Central Council for Nursing, Midwifery and Health Visiting, the General Medical Council and the boards of the Council for Professions Supplementary to Medicine.

24 Managers should encourage staff to consult with representative bodies particularly if an issue seems likely to remain unresolved without reference to the Chairman of the employing body.

The Mental Health Act Commission

25 Where an NHS employee has a concern about the care of a patient or client detained under Mental Health Act 1983, he or she may be able to refer the matter to the Mental Health Act Commission, if the concern remains unresolved after pursuing it through local procedures.

The Health Service Commissioner (The Ombudsman)

26 All staff should be made aware that the Ombudsman may look into complaints by staff on behalf of a patient, provided that he is satisfied that there is no-one more appropriate, such as an immediate relative, to act on the patient's behalf. Adequate supplies of information leaflets about the Ombudsman's role and the procedures for reference to him should be readily accessible to all staff, as well as patients.

Reference to Members of Parliament and the media

27 An employee who has exhausted all the locally established procedures, including reference to the Chairman of the employing body, and who has taken account of advice which may have been given, might wish to consult his or her Member of Parliament in confidence. He or she might also, as a last resort, contemplate the possibility of disclosing his or her concern to the media. Such action, if entered into unjustifiably, could result in disciplinary action and might unreasonably undermine public confidence in the Service.

28 In view of these considerations, any employee contemplating making a disclosure to the media is advised first to seek further specialist guidance from professional or other representative bodies and to discuss matters further with his or her colleagues and, where appropriate, line and professional managers. In the light of the principles set out in this guidance, however, and the fact that local procedures will have been determined in consultation with local staff and staff representatives, it is expected that proper mechanisms will exist to ensure that staff concerns can be addressed and dealt with without reference to the media.

REFERENCES

CLOTHIER COMMITTEE (1992) *The Ethics of Gene Therapy*. HMSO.

COMMITTEE ON HEALTH AND SAFETY AT WORK (1972) *Safety and Health at Work*: Report of the Committee 1970-72, Cmnd. 5034, Chair: Lord Robens. HMSO.

DEPARTMENT OF HEALTH (1993a) *Managing the New NHS – A Background Document*. DoH.

DEPARTMENT OF HEALTH (1993b) *Mental Health Act Code of Practice* (revised). HMSO, London.

DEPARTMENT OF HEALTH (1993c) *Legal Powers on the Care of Mentally Ill People in the Community*, Report of the Internal Review. DoH.

DEPARTMENT OF HEALTH (1994) *Being Heard*: The Report of a Review Committee on NHS Complaints Procedures. Chaired by Prof. Alan Wilson. DoH.

DEPARTMENT OF HEALTH AND SOCIAL SECURITY (1973) *Teaching on Patients*. Circular HM(73)8. DHSS.

DEPARTMENT OF HEALTH AND SOCIAL SECURITY AND WELSH OFFICE (1979) *Patients First*: A Consultative Paper on the Structure and Management of the National Health Service in England and Wales. HMSO.

EMPLOYMENT DEPARTMENT (undated) *Industrial Action and the Law*. PL 943. Employment Department.

EMPLOYMENT DEPARTMENT (undated) *Union Membership and Non-membership Rights*. PL 871 (REV3). Employment Department.

FINCH J. (1994) *Speller's Law Relating to Hospitals*. Chapman and Hall.

GLOVER J. (1977) *Causing Death and Saving Lives*. Pelican.

HARRIS J. (1985) *The Value of Life*. Routledge and Keegan Paul.

HEALTH AND SAFETY COMMISSION (1992) *Management of Health and Safety at Work*: Approved Code of Practice. HMSO.

HEALTH COMMITTEE OF THE HOUSE OF COMMONS (1993) *Community Supervision Orders*. Fifth Report, Volume 1, Session 1992-93. HMSO.

HOUSE OF LORDS (1994) *Report of Select Committee on Medical Ethics*. Session 1993-94, Volume 1. HMSO.

THE LAW COMMISSION (1991) *Mentally Incapacitated Adults and Decision-Making: An Overview*. Consultation Paper No. 119. HMSO.

THE LAW COMMISSION (1993a) *Mentally Incapacitated Adults and Decision-Making: A New Jurisdiction*. Consultation Paper No. 128. HMSO.

THE LAW COMMISSION (1993b) *Mentally Incapacitated Adults and Decision-Making: Medical Treatment and Research*. Consultation Paper No. 129. HMSO.

THE LAW COMMISSION (1993c) *Mentally Incapacitated and Other Vulnerable Adults: Public Law Protection*. Consultation Paper No. 130. HMSO.

THE LAW COMMISSION (1995) *Mental Incapacity and the draft legislation covering advanced directives*. Consultation Paper No. 231. HMSO.

THE MENTAL HEALTH ACT COMMISSION (1985) *Consent to Treatment*. The Mental Health Act Commission.

THE MENTAL HEALTH ACT COMMISSION (1993) *Fifth Biennial Report (1991-1993) of the Mental Health Act Commission*. Mental Health Act Commission.

THE NATIONAL COUNCIL OF BIOETHICS (1993) *Genetic Screening*. National Council of Bioethics.

NHS MANAGEMENT EXECUTIVE (1990) *A Guide to Consent for Examination and Treatment* (HC(90)22). DoH.

NHS MANAGEMENT EXECUTIVE (1993) *Guidance for Staff on Relations with the Public and the Media*. Circular EL(93)51. DoH.

NHS MANAGEMENT EXECUTIVE (1994) *AIDS-HIV Infected Health Care Workers: Guidance on the Management of Infected Health Care Workers*. HSG(94)16. DoH.

ROYAL COLLEGE OF PSYCHIATRISTS (1993) *Community Supervision Orders*. Royal College of Psychiatrists.

STATUTORY INSTRUMENT (1977) No. 500. *Safety Representatives and Safety Committees Regulations*. HMSO.

STATUTORY INSTRUMENT (1988) No. 1657. *The Control of Substances Hazardous to Health Regulations*. HMSO.

STATUTORY INSTRUMENT (1990) No. 2244. *Local Authority Social Services (Complaints Procedure) Order*. HMSO.

STATUTORY INSTRUMENT (1992) No. 2051. *Management of Health and Safety in the Workplace Regulations*. HMSO.

STATUTORY INSTRUMENT (1992) No. 2792. *Health and Safety (Display Screen Equipment) Regulations*. HMSO.

STATUTORY INSTRUMENT (1992) No. 2793. *The Manual Handling Operations Regulations*. HMSO.

STATUTORY INSTRUMENT (1992) No. 2932. *The Provision and Use of Work Equipment Regulations*. HMSO.

STATUTORY INSTRUMENT (1992) No. 2966. *The Personal Protective Equipment at Work Regulations*. HMSO.

STATUTORY INSTRUMENT (1992) No. 3004. *The Workplace (Health, Safety and Welfare) Regulations*. HMSO.

STATUTORY INSTRUMENT (1994) No. 2408. *The Medicinal Products: Prescription by Nurses etc. Act 1992 (Commencemnt No. 1) Order*. HMSO.

THE TIMES (1989) 'Cost of spillage from cup of tea'. The Times, 13 June.

THE TIMES (1994) 'Proving involuntary manslaughter', Law Report. The Times, July 4, p. 32.

TURNER T. (1990) 'Crushed by the system'. Nursing Times: 86 (49), p. 19.

UNITED KINGDOM CENTRAL COUNCIL FOR NURSING, MIDWIFERY AND HEALTH VISITING (1987) *Confidentiality: An Elaboration of Clause 9 of the Second Edition of the UKCC's Code of Professional Conduct for the Nurse, Midwife and Health Visitor*. UKCC.

UNITED KINGDOM CENTRAL COUNCIL FOR NURSING, MIDWIFERY AND HEALTH VISITING (1991a) *Midwives Rules*. UKCC.

UNITED KINGDOM CENTRAL COUNCIL FOR NURSING, MIDWIFERY AND HEALTH VISITING (1991b) *A Midwife's Code of Practice*. UKCC.

UNITED KINGDOM CENTRAL COUNCIL FOR NURSING, MIDWIFERY AND HEALTH VISITING (1992) *Code of Professional Conduct for the Nurse, Midwife and Health Visitor (3rd Edition)*. UKCC.

UNITED KINGDOM CENTRAL COUNCIL FOR NURSING, MIDWIFERY AND HEALTH VISITING (1993) *Standards for Records and Record Keeping*. UKCC.

WARNOCK COMMITTEE (1984) *Report of the Committee of Inquiry into Fertilisation and Embryology* (Warnock Report). Chair: Mary Warnock, Cmnd. 9314. HMSO.

WHITE PAPER (1989) *Caring for People: Community care in the next decade*. Cmnd 849, November. HMSO.

WILLIAMSON C. (1991) *Hearing Patients' Appeals Against Continued Compulsory Detention (2nd edition)*. National Association of Health Authorities and Trusts.